A HOLE
in the
OCEAN

A HOLE
in the
OCEAN

A Hamptons' Apprenticeship
& Questions After a History:
A Recapitulation

SANDY McINTOSH

MARSH HAWK PRESS
East Rockaway, New York • 2016

7 6 5 4 3 2 1 FIRST EDITION

Marsh Hawk Press books are published by Poetry Mailing List, Inc., a not-for-profit corporation under section 501(c)3 United States Internal Revenue Code.

Book Design: Susan Quasha

The author gratefully acknowledges permissions to reprint:
    "A Terrible Moon Slides Over the Roofs Like Silver Music," original letters in Dutch, translated by Philippe van Wersch, and used with permission of Philippe van Wersch and the Estate of H. R. Hays.
    "For Armand and David" used with permission of the Estate of Harvey Shapiro.
    "a letter to Paul Blackburn preceded by a letter Rainer Maria Rilke wrote 13 days before his death in 1926 to Rudolph Kassner" used with permission of the Estate of Armand Schwerner.

Library of Congress Cataloging-in-Publication Data

McIntosh, Sandy
 A hole in the ocean : a Hamptons' apprenticeship / Sandy McIntosh. —First edition.
    pages cm
 ISBN 978-0-9906669-9-8 (pbk.) —ISBN 0-9906669-9-9 (pbk.) 1. McIntosh, Sandy—Friends and associates. 2. Poets, American—20th century—Biography. 3. Art and literature—New York (State). 4. Hamptons (N.Y.)—Social life and customs. I. Title.
 PS3613.C54Z46 2015
 811'.6—dc23
 [B]
                    2015032492

Marsh Hawk Press
P.O. Box 206
East Rockaway, New York 11518-0206
www.marshhawkpress.org

Vanishing Point: In Memory of James Tate

The laws of perspective are absolute.
The road does narrow as you walk through the landscape.
This is why you see old people up ahead hobbling.
You think they are crippled by age.
But it is only that they have less space to move in.
When the lines finally converge,
they must crawl the rest of the way as if through a tunnel,
lie face down, finally, and look closer... closer...
until they have reached the Vanishing Point,
just there, at the dark edge of the eyeball.

CONTENTS

A hole in the ocean will never be missed

—e. e. cummings

A Hamptons' Apprenticeship:
Pictures from a Place and Year

INTRODUCTION

One summer evening in 1970, after my shift pumping gas, I was driving home along Springs Fireplace Road in East Hampton when I had to brake suddenly to avoid hitting a tall, thin man on a bicycle. He had swerved out of a side road, and crossed in front of me without looking. I pulled over to catch my breath. As I drew closer I recognized Willem de Kooning, whom I had met at Guild Hall during my first year at Southampton College. I watched as he rode along, pedaling uncertainly, his bike weaving figure eights from right to left. At one point he seemed to lose interest in pedaling. The bike came to a stop, stayed motionless for a moment, then pitched over to the right, its rider falling gently into the thick, uncut brush and rolling two or three times until coming to rest under some trees. I shut off my car and ran over to him. He didn't seem hurt; in fact, he was smiling pleasantly, his eyes closed as if dreaming. I touched his arm and he looked up. He was okay, he told me, but could I give him a ride home? It was getting dark and he had no light on his bicycle.

I helped him into my car and loaded the bike into the back seat. He told me to continue east and take the right fork before Barnes' grocery store. He was living in a farmhouse opposite the Green River cemetery, he said, but this was only temporary, until they finished building his new studio. "I don't want them to finish the damn thing," he said with some bitterness. I asked why not? "Because when it's finished, I think I will be finished, too."

We drove on for a few minutes until he told me to stop. "I live right here," he said. He looked in the direction of the cemetery and pointed: "All my friends are buried over there."

I was curious. I helped him out of the car and to his front door, and when he was safely inside, I crossed the road to the cemetery.

It seemed a conventional graveyard with moldering tombstones. But then I caught sight of a grave marker that was odd. It was an obsidian monolith standing about four feet high. Engraved on its face was a man's signature: the painter Stuart Davis. Looking around in that section of the cemetery, I found other oddly shaped stones, each with the name of an artist or a writer I had heard of. In front of Stuart Davis' grave was a white marble square that marked the grave of Ad Reinhardt. I discovered the flat slate grave maker of Frank O'Hara, the New York School poet who had been run over by the only vehicle on Fire Island. Inscribed on it was his quotation: "Grace to be born and live / as variously as possible." Just north of O'Hara's grave was that of the writer A. J. Liebling, the war correspondent, boxing expert, world-class eater, and, for many years at *The New Yorker*, a critic of the press. Finally, at the end of the cemetery, almost in the woods, a great boulder with a bronze plaque marked Jackson Pollock's grave. I continued on, following the horseshoe road until I came to a fence. On the other side were objects—gravestones, I thought—that were extremely weird, even grotesque, gigantic, resembling Native totem poles. I wondered about that section of the cemetery for a long time. (In fact, I learned eventually, the odd objects were not grave markers but rough carvings in the side yard of the sculptor Albert Price's house.) I visited the place often, even picnicking with friends on an artist's plot that was behind some trees, out of public view.

The cemetery was a quiet place in all seasons, and from Labor Day to Memorial Day around 1970 the noisy Hamptons' main streets were quiet, too. The only businesses open after 8:00 pm were the bars and cafes, each town supplied with one or two. Standing on Main Street, you could actually hear the crashing of ocean waves a half-mile away, a sound reverberating against the empty sidewalks and closed summer stores, surprisingly primitive and frightening.

A Secret In Plain Sight

In 1970, Southampton College, which I attended, was a college within a college. The official one advertised its original mission to serve local students, many of them children of farmers and shopkeepers who worked for the wealthy summer residents living in large homes near the Atlantic Ocean. Most of these students had practical career goals which the traditional academic faculty was tasked with assisting. Students of the unofficial college, however, those of us who had washed up on Southampton's shores with less practical plans—writing, painting and music—found another kind of faculty to help us. This one consisted of practicing artists who happened to be living in the area. Many of them, including de Kooning and Ilya Bolotowsky, had previously taught at the experimental arts college, Black Mountain. They were joined by the Bollingen Prize winning poet David Ignatow, the pioneering performance artist Charles Matz, and the polymath playwright, novelist, translator and poet H. R. Hays. How had this group coalesced? According to de Kooning, "We're here in the winter all alone. We work in our studios all day and some of us want to get together at night, usually at Bobby Van's, or some other bar. Then some people get into fights—Jim Jones likes to throw punches—or get drunk and there is trouble with the police. It's either that or we meet at the college and talk without getting into too much trouble."

The relationships my contemporaries—such as John MacWhinnie, Richard Freeman, Steven Garfield, Natasha Plotnikoff, Andrew Bolotowsky, Christopher Shaughnessy, Dan Gelfand, and Hadley Haden Guest—formed with these artists offered us more an apprenticeship than a traditional classroom-centered education. They invited us into their homes, spent long hours with us eating, drinking and talking about writing or painting or music, their own and ours. In return, we would sometimes do chores for them. That could mean driving them around, cooking meals, or, in the case of H. R. Hays, who lived in the woods but maintained a patch of lawn approximately ten feet by ten feet because he didn't want to get too far from the "suburban experience," mowing his lawn. This was the kind of artistic education based in practical and social things, mainly at the periphery of academia, not stamped by it.

The Time and Place of Poetry

The unending war in Viet Nam, with evidence of its horrendous crimes leaked daily in *The New York Times,* inspired protest poetry and marches not only in the cities but in the Hamptons, as well. Among us poets—beginners and long-published—there was excitement about what we imagined to be the looming ascendancy of poetry in America, in the American language, the language of Whitman and William Carlos Williams. One clue to its muscle, we believed, was Eugene McCarthy, a long-time member of the United States Congress from Minnesota who had run for president in 1968. He was also a poet who wrote the kind of poetry—contemporary, knowledgeable of the American tradition, intelligent—that no one had ever suspected of a politician.

Also from Minnesota, Robert Bly was causing excitement with his polemical poetry journals, *The Sixties* and *The Seventies*. He asserted that Eliot, Pound and Marianne Moore were moving away from American poetry with tremendous speed, and that a young poet could not take them for a master "without severe distortion of his own personality." Instead, Bly recommended as models the poetry of Latin America—many poets whom H. R. Hays had translated. Charles Matz created explosive "shout" poetry to confront the times. Even David Ignatow, whose small poetic song found him making plain-spoken, often personal poetic statements, issued protest manifestos, demanding "How come nobody is being bombed today?/ I want to know being a citizen/ of this country and a family man."

While many well-known painters made their year-round homes in the Hamptons, the writers I knew mostly used their Hamptons places for winter vacations and long summers, while commuting to New York City, or to teaching jobs around the country. But there seems always to have been a dedicated population of writers who, during the 1950s and 1960s focused their literary activities on the East End. H. R. Hays, often the prime mover of literary actions there, founded a magazine in 1953, *The Bonacker,* a name referring to local residents whose families had lived in the area since before the Revolutionary War. *The Bonacker's* table of contents gives a picture of the writers and artists living and working in the Hamptons at that time. These included poets, journalists, fiction writers, editors and publishers, and several who wrote scripts for the live television drama series produced in New York City. Several artists, better known for their paintings, submitted poems as well, including Larry Rivers, whose note describes him as a "Drunkard, jazz musician, painter, sculptor, writer of many long and short unpublished poems." (*For complete contributors list see* Notes.)

Although the Parrish Art Museum, East End libraries, and, increasingly, Southampton College sponsored arts events—music, painting, film and literary—the center of the local art world for decades had been Guild Hall in East Hampton. Guild Hall was well-known for its John Drew Theatre, which was often the try-out spot for plays hoping to make it to Broadway, and its art galleries, featuring local and established artists in well-organized, publicized and celebrated shows. During the `sixties and `seventies, Guild Hall became the sponsor of frequent poetry readings, and also of the Poets in the Schools program, which sent poets into local public schools to introduce poetry to school children. The benefactors of Guild Hall, guided by canny Guild Hall directors, found the money to put on first class productions in all areas of the arts. And even poets, usually the neglected painters' poor cousins, benefited from Guild Hall's attention.

Meeting H. R. Hays

H. R. Hays was a poet, translator, novelist and playwright, an historian of anthropology and zoology. His twenty-two books, reflecting the diversity of his interests, were the pioneering works in their fields. His The Dangerous Sex: the Myth of Feminine Evil, *served as respected source material for early Feminist writers. Sir Julian Huxley regarded Hays' popular history of zoology,* Birds, Beasts and Men, *as a classic of its genre. His translations of the poetry of Brecht, Vallejo, Borges, Neruda, and many others were among the first to bring these major twentieth century writers to the attention of the English-speaking world. His plays, such as* The Ballad of Davy Crockett, *were performed on Broadway. More than twenty of his shorter works appeared on television during its early days.*

I.

In my freshman year, a slip of paper inside the interoffice envelope in my student mailbox told me that Professor Hays, head of the drama department, had been assigned as my freshman advisor. I did not plan to take drama courses, so the assignment was mysterious. But since everything about college was a mystery, I headed out to keep my appointment.

Hays' office, the note told me, was backstage in the Fine Arts building. I arrived but there didn't seem to be any offices, only a few classrooms. Thinking that I was in the wrong part of the theatre, I turned toward the exit and almost ran into a tall man with thick glasses who had suddenly stepped out of what appeared to be a closet and rushed past me. A girl was sitting at a table nearby and I asked her who that had been. She told me it was Professor Hays. I asked where his office was and she told me that it was there, in that closet.

I caught up with him in the parking lot where he was fumbling with his keys. I introduced myself as his advisee and told him I'd arrived for our appointment.

"Ah," he said, fuming. "That was the last straw! Did you know the janitor has now been authorized to store his buckets, mops and brooms in my office? They promised me a real office when the new building was finished. Now they say I just have to 'make do', whatever that means. Next they'll have me working out of a stall in the men's room!"

"Should we make another appointment, when it's more convenient for you?" I asked, because I didn't know what else to say.

"Well, we can talk here for a few minutes. What are you?"

"What am I?"

"I mean, are you a playwright, a director, a scenic designer? What?"

"Actually, I'll probably be an English major."

"You don't want to write plays?"

"Well, I would like to write plays. Mostly I write poetry. Sometimes short stories."

"What poets do you like?"

I had discovered Eliot's "The Love Song of J. Alfred Prufrock," and though I didn't quite understand it, I loved the way it sounded when I'd read it aloud. I'd read it so many times that I'd memorized it. I told Hays about this and he ordered me to recite. I gave him the first few stanzas.

"That's enough. You're like a lot of these modern poets: they just mumble their words into their beard or down their shirts. I teach a Public Speaking class next semester. Why don't you sign up for it? You'll learn to declaim properly."

He found the correct car key. "Come and see me again and bring some of your poetry. I write poetry myself."

He drove off and I was left with a campus that seemed abandoned, the students and professors having gone to more populous, exciting areas for the weekend. That afternoon, H. R. Hays had seemed an angry, forlorn figure in a lonely landscape. Few students I'd spoken with had met him or even heard of him, though he taught a full course load. To those who acknowledged knowing him, Hays remained a mystery, an odd duck, an almost-invisible man.

II. There Were Too Many Painters In My Family

"There were too many painters in my family. I decided to become a poet," Hays told me. Indeed, his grandfather, W. J. Hays became a widely recognized painter of the Old West.

Of him Hays wrote:

> In 1861 my grandfather
> Dipped his brushes in the frontier,
> Sat by the stockades
> On the Missouri River
> Sketching Indians.

His great-grandfather, Jacob, was the first Chief Constable of New York City. Another relative, was publisher of *The New York Times*.

Hays' father, W. J. Jr. grew up in New York City, but preferred the country, surrounded by animals. Like his father, he was a painter, but without a sense of adventure or curiosity for travel.

Of him Hays wrote:

> My father lived with horses,
> He was embarrassed by words
> And wanted to
> Paint himself into a world
> That didn't exist.

Hoffman Hays had published poetry during his undergraduate years at Cornell and while he completed his Masters of Arts at Columbia University. By 1929 he had written enough finished poetry to publish a collection, *Strange City*. The poems in it are pleasant, traditional verse. "Well," Hays said. "I no longer have any copies of that book and we will not speak of it."

Hays wanted a radical change in his life. He was 25 years old. He had arranged a place for himself at the University of Liege in Belgium and secured passage aboard a cargo ship for Holland.

III. A Terrible Moon Slides Over the Roofs Like Silver Music

For the next year Hays traveled through Holland, Luxembourg and France. Early in the year, visiting Brussels, he met a young woman named Cara von Wersch, known as Corrie. She was nineteen, a student at the Catholic Social School for Women. Since both of them had an interest in the theater, it is probable that they met in that milieu. They developed a romantic relationship over the year, and Hays's letters to her in Dutch reveal private sentiments that even those who knew him best as an English speaker later on might never have heard. Early in the year he writes to her:

> The strange electricity that can attract you to a certain being, that makes me desire to show you your inner self—and what a lovely mood! Can one with something like this overcome all obstacles, practical situations and differences of ideas? I'd like to try it…. I write you no romantic promises but I fight to reach what I believe exists, that perhaps can be very important. I've tried a few times to find the way to somebody, without success. I don't know if it is possible.

> I have too often killed my own feelings by analyzing too much. Look how badly I follow my own theory, saying this to tell you "I love you." Writers are awful people, Corrie. They cannot write a love letter with style. They always give only a part of themselves to somebody, the rest always remains the artist.

He felt comfortable writing in Dutch, though he had only recently learned the language. He may have felt protected by its foreignness when writing such intimate stuff. Corrie's nephew, Phillipe von Wersch, who translated the letters for me, marveled at Hays's command of the language: "I wonder where he learned to write such splendid Dutch. Some words certainly have poetic sounds. Without these poetic sounds in mind one couldn't translate these letters."

On May 4th he was stopping at a hotel in Paris on the rue du Calvaire. The hotel is on a square that offers a panoramic view of the Paris streets and rooftops. He writes:

A terrible moon slides over the roofs like silver music. It is warm. People sit in cafes and seem to be satisfied. The night appears to me as something very old and slithery and I am not hers. I've almost lived a year without people, I mean without intimate relations with people, but no one needs people more than I do. You don't know what it is, wanting to be an artist. You place your work above your own happiness and then if the mood is bad you feel that you have done nothing; you criticize everything and don't trust yourself. I keep myself busy with all sorts of problems, Communism, the individual and the society—craziness.

He is happy to be in Holland:

I have always felt in you something in the Dutch character that I love. It is something I actually look for in my friends: imagination, feeling that we are in a world of miracles where anything can happen ... Opinions, systems of down-to-earth people are precious to me ... In my opinion, real education should train athletes of the spirit. These we need now against the materialism, against the "defeatism," against the whole mess of our modern society.

And he is pleased with Luxembourg:

People paint the houses in light colors of brown and rose, a remarkable difference between Belgium and Luxemburg and I feel also a bit more Germanic in the people—not only in their language—it's a way of doing everything nicely. It is strange if you think how undisturbed such a small country could stay, apparently without any real nationalist feeling.

The lack of nationalist feeling in the Netherlands, especially in Holland, Hays attributed to their abstention from fighting in the recent World War. In a summative article in *The New Review*, published in Paris in 1931, he theorizes:

The literary output in Holland is not overvital. One has the impression of an old and rich culture gone temporarily stale.... Holland abstained from the war, and she has also abstained from the anarchy of modernism in the arts, which seems to be vitally connected with that catharsis of blood and fire. Always conservative, she is still trying to preserve her balance with the old philosophies.

By the middle of the next year he is thinking of his return to America:

Little by little I get the desire to see New York. Our climate is totally different from the Netherlands: dry, warm and a lot of sun. I suffered a lot from the dreary winter of Europe and I believe that a certain American optimism is totally the results of our climate. Do you love the sun? I'm fanatic about it and a terrible nudist. The physical life in America is free with a certain careless grace. (I find the bourgeois dignity of Holland disgusting.)

I would love to make a fusion of our ways of life and the European soul. Yet I place our intellect higher than the European. I don't know; no rose without thorns. I find the superstitious [religious] beliefs of Europe a source of unhappiness. No, we should have a new kind of religion, little by little build up something that will have an emotional value and yet that won't go against scientific facts and modern intelligence....

His short article in the *New Review* Vol. 1, No. 1, which was edited by the American author and translator Samuel Putnam, along with help from Ezra Pound, Maxwell Bodenheim, and Richard Thoma, gives short shrift to what he perceives as the lack of life in contemporary Dutch literature:

The prose fares worse than the poetry. Holland's own critics complain that the recent novel is hopelessly local. A degenerate naturalism analyses ad nauseam the woes of sex-starved spinsters ... and there is not much of international interest....

The poetry is more sensitive to outside influences. Then, too, Holland has always had a fine poetic tradition. A Catholic renaissance, undoubtedly influenced and stimulated by the neo-medievalism of Flanders, with Utrecht as the center, can boast a few tender psalmists....

On the whole, one feels a withdrawal from, rather than an acceptance of life. Holland awaits a new movement, a house-cleaning, a readjustment to the exigencies of the future.

This assessment is as terse, forceful and intellectually rigid as any twenty-five-year-old's literary challenge might be, but his discussions of the characteristics and importance of Dutch writers show that he'd read deeply in the literature. At the same time, his terseness and forcefulness seem the natural voice of one who has not only lived the last year alone, but someone often at life-long odds with his circumstances. As he laments to Corrie on May 24th from Paris:

If I had somebody here with me with whom I was intimate I would finish it all by speaking. I am alone and so I write. Why? Because I always have words, words, words and more words.

On July 9th he writes to Corrie announcing that he will leave for America from Antwerp aboard the Westland of the Red Star Line. He tells her that her last letter to him, in which she apparently confessed her love for him, made him very happy:

Even the fact that I'm departing rapidly for the other end of the earth can't sober me and I don't know how I shall collect myself enough to get my packing done. And this had to happen just when I'm leaving and Lord knows how much time before I can see you again! You sweet child!

But in his next letter, written aboard the Westland, he reveals that his feelings have changed. He has met a Dutch girl who will be studying ballet somewhere in the U.S., and he has fallen in love with her. Under the circumstances, he says, all is now over between Corrie and himself. ("My

22

aunt didn't save this letter, Phillip von Wersch writes in 2002, "but she told someone about it. And I spoke to this woman last week.") After the crossing, the dancer never heard from Hays again.

After Corrie's death in November 2000, her nephew found Hays's letters, carefully preserved, as well a copy of his poetry collection, *Strange City*, in her attic. He'd inscribed the book to her: "A piece of my youth which shines far in the past."

IV. Ability With Languages

"I've always had ability with languages, I suppose," he said. When I asked how he'd learned Dutch on his own—not in a classroom—he answered off-handedly: "Oh, the usual way. I bought a grammar and read through it, and I was all set." That is to say, he read through a language teaching text, grabbing the essentials of the language all at once. He also learned not only the grammars but the idioms of French, German, Dutch and Spanish on his own from grammar texts and a deep reading of the countries' literature, as well as from traveling where the languages were spoken.

Reading widely in these languages, he discovered poetry that excited him. If there was any poetry to compare it to it was Walt Whitman's, and not the contemporary American poetry derived from English poets and their tradition. In the next decades he translated and published work by Spanish American poets, including Pablo Neruda, César Vallejo, and others, as well as the poetry of Bertolt Brecht, little of which was known in America.

Like Hays' Brecht translations, *12 Spanish American Poets* has endured in print, despite the multiplicity of other translators reconsidering the same work. Hays' explanation for the longevity of his translations was simple: "I just think, when you translate, you ought to let your readers know what the poet says. A lot of translators don't believe in this approach: they prefer to put down what they think the poet ought to have said."

Oddly, it was Robert Bly, another poet-translator, the veracity of whose translations has been challenged, who praised Hays' pioneering work and brought Hays' own original poetry, now infused with a strong Latin-American surrealism, to public notice. Bly had been enthusiastic about Hays' translations. He wrote: "When I was trying to write my first book, I found the most amazing things in the ... New York Public Library on 42nd St., and one of the most astonishing to me was H. R. Hays' *12 Spanish American Poets.*"

He was also enthusiastic about Hays' own poetry when he wrote: "This book is a mountain pass.... I am grateful to H. R. Hays for so many gifts, in prose and poetry."

V. An Early Lesson

During my final years in boarding school I had been writing poetry and compiling it in a thick loose-leaf notebook. I had shown some of my poetry to Hays and he had been encouraging. I arrived at his home for a poetry party and reading and was immediately daunted by the size of the crowd. Certainly I was the youngest. Several poets preceded me, and when it was my turn I read the poem of mine that Hays had selected. Afterwards, the applause surprised and pleased me. Before I could sit down, someone asked me to read another. Others in the audience applauded. Flattered, I reopened my notebook looking for an appropriate encore. Time passed; the audience grew restive. As I flipped to the end of the notebook I panicked. I had seen an ugly, looming truth. Not one of those poems was any good!—a devastating realization that I had been deceiving myself all along, carrying around an impressive folder filled with what I now realized was self-indulgent crap. Nevertheless, I couldn't let the audience know about this. Thinking hard, I remembered I had recently written something that was more promising than my usual. I laboriously turned the pages searching for it, even though I sensed I was losing the audience. In the end, refusing to admit a truth that was nobody's business but mine, I took the chance and recited the poem from memory. The response amazed me. Everyone seemed to be laughing and applauding. Later, Hays introduced me to Allen Planz, who was then Poetry Editor of the *Nation*. He invited me to submit the poem to that magazine. It was only after I was back in the anonymity of the audience that I realized I had omitted to recite most of the poem's lines. Somehow, panic had edited me, cutting the inferior lines and leaving only the poem's true heart. It was a fundamental lesson.

VI. Home Life with Hoffman and his wife, Julie: A Video Record

I had been interviewing Hays on video one afternoon about his association with Bertolt Brecht, whose plays and poetry he'd translated. In return, Brecht had translated one of Hays' poems into German.

"Brecht was a son of a bitch," Hays declared. "He had the most annoying habit of granting exclusive world rights to the translation of his plays to several people at once, and of course he never let any of them know he was doing it. Then, as always happened, one of them would catch on, and some ridiculous fiasco would ensue."

"This translation," Hays said, "has a rather pronounced Brechtian character—as does everything that Brecht touched, of course."

HAYS: It was one of the poems I wrote during the War. I took it from a story in the newspaper that talked about the sale of pulp fiction mysteries and romances in England. It seems sales dipped on any day that there were bombings. It was obvious to me that people who liked to read that gory stuff, which they had to pay something like five cents a copy for, understood that they could get the real gore for free, just by looking out their windows. (*Begins to read the poem in German, but stumbles over the words.*)

JULIE: You should have practiced reading it before you started recording.

HAYS: Yes. Well, it's nice to know that after the fact. Can we do it again? Okay. (*Begins reading from the beginning.*)

JULIE: (*from the kitchen*) What do you want to do about the potatoes?

HAYS: (*stops reading, looks up silently, then continues reading.*)

JULIE: (*interrupting*): Oh for God's sake! This is….

HAYS: (*over his shoulder, annoyed*) This is fine.

JULIE: Well, it hasn't been basted and it's drying on the outside….

HAYS: All right. So baste it. And don't have a fit.

JULIE: Well, I had no idea anything was cooking in here, Hoffman.

HAYS: I told you I was cooking dinner. Everything is always my fault. (*Continues reading in German. Background sounds from the kitchen of water running. Hays raises his voice to read the last lines over the even louder sounds of something being roughly chopped.*)

JULIE: (*still in the kitchen*) Oh God damn it! This is all wrong!

HAYS: (*finishes reading with a triumphant smile; looks at the camera*) Well, did you get that all right this time?

David Ignatow: Notes On A Small Song

*Born in 1914 to Russian emegré parents, Ignatow grew up in
Brooklyn without much money, but with a single-minded desire to
write. Like other writers who came of age during the Depression
years, Ignatow was engaged in social issues. He worked at menial
jobs and in WPA projects, edited an activist literary review, and
was briefly a member of the Young Communist League. With the
publication of his first book, Poems in 1948, he began to earn
his reputation as a poet oriented to the life of the city. He was the
author of eighteen volumes of poetry and three of prose. While I
knew him, he received Yale's Bollingen Prize, two Guggenheim
fellowships, the Wallace Stevens Award, the Shelley Memorial, an
award from the Nation Institute of Arts and Letter, and the Robert
Frost, John Steinbeck and William Carlos Williams awards.*

I.

When he bought his house near Barnes Landing, Ignatow said, "Here
I am. I've come to join the exiles." He was a city boy, and the
trees surrounding his country house made him uneasy. "They're like pris-
on bars."

He'd tried to understand this new place. He wrote poems. One began,
"About my being a poet, the trees certainly haven't expressed an interest,
standing at a distance. I'd expect that at least they'd try to learn some-
thing new besides growing their leaves...."

II.

Sitting in the woods across the picnic table from him I said: "My last year in
boarding school, I hid in my dorm room and read more than 1,000 books!"

"What?" He winced, putting down his forkful of tinned salmon. "You
actually read 1,000 books in one year?"

"Well, perhaps, not a thousand…." In fact, I'd meant, I'd read maybe fifty or sixty books.

"Fifty, sixty or 1,000?" he demanded. "Which is it?"

Why should he care? I'd said "1,000" for effect, the way medieval historians reported the casualties on the battlefield. If I didn't care about the exact number, why should he?

But he frowned as if I'd hurt him. "How can you use language so irresponsibly?" he wanted to know.

"Well," I retorted, "you write in your poem, 'This tree has two million and seventy-five thousand leaves. Perhaps I missed a leaf or two…' You're not going to tell me you actually did the counting. Maybe my books are like your trees."

"Impossible. You want me to believe that you read a specific number of books in a year. My exaggeration is a higher truth; yours is just a lie. Anyway, a writer uses language at all times forcefully, saying exactly what is intended, nothing more. Why don't you understand that?"

III.

I stopped off at his house with a new poem I wanted him to see.

"He's teaching at the college today," said his wife. "But come sit at the typewriter and wait for him."

In the next room I could hear a radio announcing the death of General Eisenhower. She was surprised. "I thought he'd been dead for years."

We listened together as the announcer read off a list of complex funerary events. She remarked on how chilling it all was. "They couldn't wait for him to drop dead."

That gave me an idea. She encouraged me to use her typewriter. "Go ahead," she said. "Type all you want."

My father had admired Eisenhower and always voted Republican. At his death I'd been fascinated with the preparations for the funeral, especially the process of embalming the corpse. I was thinking as much of my own father's funeral as of Eisenhower's while I worked at the typewriter.

Ignatow returned from teaching in an acrimonious mood. After supper (canned salmon on dry lettuce; water), he motioned me to hand him the poem.

I gave him the one I'd arrived with, something I'd worked on for weeks. This, I wanted him to know, was finally the real thing.

He made chomping sounds, cleaning his teeth with his tongue as he read. When he looked up it was with a sour expression. "This is crap," he pronounced. "Why are you wasting your time with this garbage? You can write better than that."

I was devastated. I couldn't breathe. I felt as if he'd shoved me backwards through the wall; that I was being pinned to the menacing trees in his angry forest.

"Come on," he chided. "You can talk. You're not going to die."

But I couldn't talk, his condemnation so forceful, unexpected. To play for time, I opened my notebook and offered up the new poem I'd written about Eisenhower. It wasn't much. I'd just been having fun with it. But that's all I had.

He grabbed it. His expression softened and he looked up from the type-written sheet. "Now, this is something," he said. "This should be published. Why didn't you show me this the first time?"

IV.

He asked me to help with a poetry magazine he was editing. The manuscript pile was daunting. We waded through it for many hours. Later, at dinner, I suggested we go to an open poetry reading at the Whaling Museum.

"Aw, come on," he sighed. "Do you really want to go to some reading after all the crap I've made you look at today? Okay. We'll go. But if I don't like it, I'll give you a signal and we'll leave."

I was surprised at his attitude. Having arrived at our destination, he led me to the back of the gallery, to seats nearest the exit. "The best seats in the house," he confided, eying the exit door.

He held court until the first reader reached the podium. Several young poets came up to him for autographs and blessings. The lights went down and he tugged at my sleeve. "I've had enough," he whispered. "Let's go."

"But no one's read yet."

"All right. You stay. I'll meet you back at the house."

He glided to the door; a silent, practiced exit.

When I returned he was sitting outdoors on the patio with a pile of manuscripts. "You know," he observed, dumping the pile into the trash-can. "There are more people in the world writing poetry than have ever read a poem."

V.

"I regard this poet as if he were my own son," he once wrote recommending me for a teaching job.

Then once, at three in the morning, when I found I had no place to sleep, I inched my car down his rocky drive, being as quiet as I could, intending to sleep in the trees, but the tires on gravel made a racket.

"What do you think you're doing?" he hissed, holding a flashlight to the car window. "You've scared us half to death. Get the hell out of here and don't come back until you're sober!"

VI.

Allen Ginsberg was reading at the library. In his old age, even a modest staircase was impossible for Ignatow. I'd driven him to the library, but we'd need someone to help get him up and through the door. Happily, Ginsberg was getting out of someone's car. Between us we hoisted Ignatow over the steps, our arms interlaced in a fireman's carry.

Ignatow's health continued to decline. Yet one day I saw him walking down Main Street, smiling and waving at people in the shops. "What's happened to you?" I asked.

"The doctors," he told me. "It's a new medication. I feel great!" Indeed, the next time I saw him he was driving his car, running a traffic light.

One afternoon I brought him the news: Allen Ginsberg had died.

"Ah," he answered. "That's too bad. But then he was quite elderly, wasn't he?"

VII.

Ignatow was dying, laid out in a rented hospital bed in his writing room. He turned to me and said, "I'm here to die."

I didn't know how to answer, so I looked out the window at the trees.

He joined me in silence for a few moments. "I'm enjoying the view," he said. "I finally understand the trees. They're like the crib I slept in as a child. They won't let me fall to the ground."

Finally I asked if there was anything I could do for him.

He thought for a bit. "Yes," he answered with his sly smile. "Trade places with me."

VIII.

When it was over, technicians used a bone saw to remove his brain. His doctors wanted to study the effects of the disease that killed him. "I imagine it will be a big operation, bright lights, medical students watching," Ignatow had told me. But, in the end, it was quick, non-dramatic: Two men alone, going about their work, efficient valets unpacking the contents of a modest suitcase.

Charles Matz: Chaos

Charles Matz came to the college from teaching at Notre Dame. He began performing his "shout" poetry—an antecedent of the larger genre called performance poetry—at Notre Dame, having been invited by his students to shake things up at a rock concert. He recalled that the rehearsal was raucous, "the clamber of noise extraordinary. I reasoned that I would have to create something that would match or exceed their volume level. The performance was before many rather staid nuns and priests. They were absolutely stunned. I had the students turn up the volume to blast people." Despite his passion for performance, he continued to teach literature in Europe, England and the United States. In a diverse creative life he also held the post of iconographer of nave clerestory windows, Washington National Cathedral.

I. Peace Cry

A friend introduced us. "I think you two might like each other," she said outside his office.

"Come into the office," Professor Matz said. "I want you to hear something."

He said he had written a poem for the next day's campus protest against the Vietnam War. He lifted the manuscript from his desk, looked at me, lifted his right arm dramatically and shouted:

Salve
  Salve
We!
  we we we
     We!

gathered gat got
hear here we

are for
for gathered
for
not nothing
we here gathered
nothing
we can say here
no thing no no No!

He lowered his arm and his voice. "That's how it begins," he said. "What do you think?"

The suddenness of his vocal attack had pinned me to the chair. What did I think? What the hell was he doing? "You're going to read that at the rally, Professor?"

"Yes. Shouldn't I? You think it outlandish?"

"I think it's, uh, dangerous."

"Ah ha!" he shouted. "Exactly right!"

The next day, at 2:30 in the afternoon, Rita Scholl, a mutual friend, and I stood outside on the flag stone assembly area. There was a good size crowd.

Rita later wrote: "The kids milled around as they will on such a warm fall day, only halfheartedly listening to the procession of speakers. "And now Dr. Matz will read his 'Peace Cry'." When I heard the beginning of it, I panicked for him. No—it was too emotional, the kids would laugh. Why did he do it? Why risk exposing so much of himself? But, perceptively, the milling and the chatter stopped. We were caught up in that raw emotion. He could not be ignored. The pain was too obvious. The poem with its repetitions, foreign sounds, shouts, Latin phrases and words laid bare the whole frustration and anger we all felt for the futility and the stupidity of the war. We were swept along responding to the cries of pain, relieved to be able to hear someone screaming for us things we could never say in quite the same way."

At the end, there was an enthusiastic ovation, the poet, exhausted, retreated backstage, unable to acknowledge the acclaim.

I was emotional too. Matz' performance had indeed been outlandish, but it had captured and tamed the audience.

And, as singular as his performance had been, there was something familiar about it, as well. It reminded me of the Saturdays when my aunt had taken me, as a young kid, to the Metropolitan Opera in New York City. I'd seen the most outlandish singing actors strutting about the stage in over-the-top melodrama. But I'd also seen their performances veer into something luminous beyond the theater, the story, the costumes and the calendar. This is what we'd seen Matz do alone on the makeshift stage: by putting himself on the line with everything he had, he'd transcended that tedious campus space and taken us across that line. This wasn't mere theatricality. This was opera.

In fact, Matz had been intimately involved with opera, especially at the Metropolitan Opera in New York City, since a child. He met his wife, Mary Jane Phillips, at Columbia University. She had trained as an amateur light soprano and was the assistant editor of *Opera News* published by the Met. Matz and Mary Jane had translated Italian opera libretti during the 1950s and '60s. While both had been born in America—Mary Jane in Ohio and Charles in New Jersey—their interests weren't limited by American geography.

In this way, Matz differed from Hays and Ignatow. Hays, who spoke several European languages and had traveled widely, always returned to the U.S. Ignatow's family had emigrated from Europe and both his parents' and his own interest was intensely focused on securing a place in this country. While Ignatow and Hays were followers of contemporary American poets, especially William Carlos Williams, who wrote in a declared American English, Matz's concerns were international and eclectic, more like those of Ezra Pound than of Williams'.

II. Chaos

Right before Christmas, Matz told me he had to leave for Italy, permanently. His rental house corridors were filled with packing boxes. I had to climb over things to get in.

Matz said he was ready to go. He'd quit his teaching job in the middle of the semester. "It's my wife's fault. She can't stay another year in this benighted country, with this war going on. She's fled to Venice, demanding I follow before scandal overtakes them. She's mad, you know. Gone 'round the twist. Someone must stop her. (He pretends to draw a knife, snarls) "*Un coltello affilato!*" he shouts. (Then wistful) "Oh, for a sharp knife! "But, absent that, I'll drop everything—as always."

In class, we'd studied Norman Mailer's novel, *An American Dream*. Matz had explained it: "Rojack feels the weight of his guilt not only because he's murdered his wife, but, a man cursed with freedom, he feels the guilt of the world on his shoulders, and he must have redemption. Rojack's father-in-law forces him out onto the building's ledge thirty stories up. For redemption Rojack must walk 'round the building's ledge following the other's commands.

"It's absurd," said Matz. "Yes, but like Rojack, I myself must travel from one place to another, walking up and down the earth, round the high and frightening building ledges, for my sins, for what the world has sinned Through me."

"What has the world sinned through you? What have you done?" I asked.

"Love," he whispers. "Only I, loving, lonely, unloved."

We drank wine. Soon the taxi arrived to take him to the airport.

"Rojack walks into the desert," Matz continued. "He finds a telephone. He calls his true love, Cherry."

His overnight bag in hand, Matz opened the front door and stood in the walkway. He turned to me. While the fall morning sun shone on him, obliterating his features, he declaimed the final lines of Cherry's big speech:

> But now it's toodle-oo, old baby-boy,
> And keep the dice for free.
> The moon is out … (*He shouts to the sky: "The moon is out!"*)
> And she's a mother
> To me!

Then, an afterthought, as the cab begins to roll down the driveway, his last words: "Hate to leave a mess. But, well, there it is."

III. Exile in Italy

Matz lived in Northern Italy and Liguria for twelve years, teaching at universities, founding a language school and giving poetry performances, once in a massive hydro-electric generator plant during a lighting storm.

I visited him twice, in Feltre and another time in San Remo. I'd studied Italian so I could get around and be on something of an equal footing with him, since he often zigged and zagged in his relationships.

In Venice, he was surprised—astonished—to find that his neighbors were Ezra Pound and Olga Rudge, who had been living there since shortly after Pound's return from St. Elizabeth's Hospital in 1958. (When asked the date of his release from the mental hospital, Pound had replied: "I never was. When I left the hospital I was still in America, and all America is an insane asylum.") In any event, he and Matz became friends. Matz' young daughter, Clare, often played chess with Pound.

Matz attended Pound's funeral.

From the ski slopes at Cortina d'Ampezzo on, December 3, 1972, Matz wrote that Pound's funeral was grim, that he had insisted on the bitterest kind of ceremony: "The coffin on the floor of the church, no flowers nearby, a single candle." There were perhaps only one or two Americans present. "Only his daughter wept." A Roman Catholic Mass was conducted, followed by an Anglican benediction.

> I had been ill with depression the night he died and knew later why. A week or so ago I spent 6 hours with him, he was in bed, bitter and caustic. He only relaxed when we talked of his friend Gaudier-Breska the sculptor dead in 1914 of the war. Clare Matz cried when she heard the news but few others. He is gone. Too bad. I liked Pound.

IV. Later: The Brutality of Memory

I recited to Charles Matz opening lines of his unfinished memoir, as I recalled them from years before: "The last time I saw Peggy Guggenheim in Venice she was pushing furniture out her palazzo window into the canal below. 'It is too ugly!' she was shouting. 'È *troppo bruto!*'"

"Hold it right there!" Matz ordered me. "I did not write that."

I hadn't spoken with him in fifteen years. When I'd looked him up I'd found him after those years of living and teaching in Italy, again at Long Island University, but at the Brooklyn campus because Southampton had been sold to the State University. I was at work on this project and was happy to have at least one of my former teachers alive and available to me.

"You've turned the incident on its head! What actually occurred was that, anticipating Peggy Guggenheim's visit, we—my wife and my children—were desperately searching the canal embankments for some discarded chairs and tables with which we might furnish our apartment. That's how poor we were. And what else have you turned around and upside-down in your recollections?" he said. "Think on those things you've written about Hays, Ignatow, Bolotowsky, Wheelock, and the others. Are you sure they're true?"

I was suddenly chilled by doubt.

He held up the paper so I could see the writing. "You've even got my name wrong!" And I could see that I'd written "Charles MAX."

"My name is not MAX!"

Rhea Is Dead

I.

After an errand, I stopped at Rhea's and Peter's studio. Without knowing it, I was barging in on a fight. "Never mind how many girlfriends I have," Peter was assailing Rhea, who was red from crying. "I've worked hard and I deserve as many as I want."

When I'd first met them at an art show at Guild Hall, they were sharing a studio in a small house, a roll of blank canvas six or eight feet high and fifteen feet long hanging from the ceiling, separating their work spaces. Rhea had begun as a painter, occasionally writing a short story and even a novel, but painting was what she enjoyed most. However, Peter was against it. "There is room for only one painter in this house," he declared. So while Peter painted on his side of the curtain, Rhea wrote her stories in longhand, so that the sound of typing wouldn't annoy her husband.

One story she wrote was about a lady writer living in a basement in a city. The lady did not do much writing because she was caught in indecision. Sitting in her armchair in the darkest corner of the basement, she debated how she could meet the outside world on terms that would permit her to be at her best. It wasn't fame, or money, or even recognition she wanted.

There was always noise in the street where the lady writer worked. A store might be robbed, a child might be hit by a car, or a man might collapse on the ground. The lady writer hardly permitted herself to pay much attention to these events, since she resented the gawkers, the idly curious. But as time passed, her attention began to turn to the outside world. There was something about these happenings that called to her. Not prurient voyeurism, certainly, but the pain these people were expressing. It was the pain she recognized that called to her. She would write about their pain.

II.

Peter knew his Mitteleuropean accent was so distinctive he never announced his name over the phone. "It's Rhea, my wife," he growled. "She died. There wasn't anything I could do about it."

I was vacationing down the Island, so I packed some clothes and started the long drive to his home. He'd asked—demanded—that I help him with his wife's funeral, "and all things someone must do to bury a dead woman." This trip had been easier, I reflected, when I'd lived a few miles from him—not hours—and he could wake me in the middle of the night knowing that I'd rush over if he suddenly needed his lawn mowed.

"I heard her coughing," he had told me. "It sounded as if she couldn't breathe. I didn't pay much attention; she often sounds this way. Then she calls my name. 'What is wrong?' I ask her, but she doesn't answer."

After years of dispute between them, they had moved into opposite wings of their home, a locked door demarcating their habitations. Peter continued: "I unlock the door and walk into the hall. She is around the corner collapsed on her bed. No more talking. I call the fire department. They send the ambulance. They take her away."

Although Peter had become a successful abstract painter, his work shown at prestigious New York galleries, he had been born poor and somehow carried that tattered suitcase with him throughout his life, even to the great, personally-designed home he'd finally arrived at. "I was impoverished," he had explained to me during an evening meal. "When you have no money you use the talents you have to make your way in the world."

Rhea had been sitting in her usual place, a low chair in the shadows, away from the table. "Tell him about your grand talent," she said.

"Well, I could paint, of course," Peter continued. "The great Hans Hoffman told my mother, 'Your son has lots of talent; he will be a painter. But make from him an overall cultured man who knows languages and knows all the music, poetry, painting, and etcetera.' That is the secret," he told me, "that you have to have an acquaintance with the world."

"Did you learn other languages?" I asked.

39

"He did not," Rhea interjected.

"Learning to speak this language was difficult enough. But I did make an acquaintance with the world."

"Tell this boy your talents," Rhea insisted.

"I have charm, I think," he suggested.

"Hmmph!" Rhea snorted. "Yes, and he formed an acquaintance with the women on the grant committees, the curators of museums, the gallery women. And he used his great talent that he carries in his pants to charm them. They show his paintings. They bring buyers to him—women buyers for him to charm. And they all make money! All of them…" Rhea then listed the influential women who allegedly did Peter's bidding on his road to fame, and dismissed each with a scatological parody of her name.

I stayed with Peter for two weeks, during which time we buried his wife, though not in the expensive artists' cemetery where Peter owned a plot for himself, but in town, in the public cemetery for the locals and the help.

During that time, as visitors arrived to offer condolences, he'd tell them the story of Rhea's death. But in each telling, I noticed, the staging changed. The story progressed from the colorless set of actions in the version he gave me, to a pageant of some drama: "She died in my arms, you know," he would announce solemnly, sounding the words, finding their balance. "She died in my arms. I was right there with her."

A couple of weeks later, I sent him a short poem in which I believed I'd painted a playful, pleasing picture of their relationship. Immediately after receiving it he was on the phone to me shouting: "I never beat my wife! Not once did I beat her!" I thought he must be drinking again.

The next time I drove out to see him he was in his studio working on a large canvas. He seemed much recovered. He was famous for his fierce depictions of women, but the woman on this new canvas, tall, well-proportioned, radiated a kind of classical beauty. He painted with great energy. He seemed once more the flamboyant painter of renown. "You see," he pointed with a wide smile. "It is Rhea, emerging from the clouds. And that male figure in the background? That is I, Poseidon, emerging from the ocean. Together she and I complete the earth and sky. This is my memorial to our love."

Disquieting as I found this scene, it fit with a lesson he'd attempted to teach one night after dinner, some months before Rhea's death. He had spoken to me with great sincerity, saying, "Despite your bourgeois upbringing, your father's money, you live in spiritual poverty. And whatever I, a poor man, give to you, you snap it up ravenously, as if it were your first meal this month. You are so hungry you make a poor man believe he is a great benefactor. So I want you to understand how we poor men must raise ourselves. It is not merely the physical," he continued, with a nod to Rhea. "If you have nothing you have to be your own benefactor. You have to sculpt your life. At every moment you must seize your situation. You must leave the ordinary world that embraces only failure, and enter the world of the great artists; you must construct for yourself a mythology."

John Hall Wheelock: A Brief Return

Wheelock had been a celebrated poet in the first half of the 20th century, a winner of Yale's Bollingen Prize for Poetry, and—fascinating to me—an editor at Scribner's publishing house. Along with his senior, Maxwell Perkins, Wheelock was responsible for discovering and fostering the talents of Ernest Hemingway, F. Scott Fitzgerald, and many other novelists and poets, including May Swenson.

I.

"You will excuse me," the elderly poet said as he adjusted the pince-nez glasses before examining the book I'd offered. "I misplaced my new glasses. I suppose these look rather silly, but in my time they were an essential part of a gentleman's costume."

Wheelock asked what writers I'd read. I told him I'd spent my teen years reading biographies of authors, and about my pursuit of a favorite British writer, P. G. Wodehouse, that began with a trip to England to meet him and, when I found he wasn't there, ended with a visit to his actual home in Remsenburg, just west of Westhampton.

Wheelock said, "You know, I had a similar experience. When I was at Harvard I fell in love with the poetry of Algernon Swinburne. Unlike you younger poets, in around 1907 we were deeply in love with rhyme. And even though English is not the most facile language for producing rhymes, Swinburne was able to work magic, producing three, four or even five rhymes within the same verse line. And all of them sounded so natural!"

Wheelock's admiration for Swinburne was so great that he convinced his father to pay for his passage to England so that he could introduce himself to the great poet. Once in London, he found Swinburne's address and, not having brought with him a letter of introduction, could only wait outside for several days, hoping that Swinburne would show himself.

On the third day, Swinburne appeared, walking toward his building. Wheelock, gathering his courage, approached him but couldn't speak. "Swinburne had an extravagant reputation that he, no doubt, worked hard at. Oscar Wilde had said about him that, though he affected to be a great homosexual and bestializer, there was nothing either foppish or bestial about him. In fact, Swinburne turned out to be a little man, conservatively dressed, and without the flamboyant hair waving in the breeze that his portraits depicted. Even so, I hadn't the courage to speak to him. I managed only to touch his coat as he passed in the street. I spent the rest of the day in my hotel room lying on the bed, thinking about the great man."

II.

In Hays' library there were several of Wheelock's poetry collections and I borrowed them. My idea was to get to know them before our next meeting. Reading, though, I was immediately overwhelmed by what I took to be gushing sentimentality—something contemporary writers I admired rooted out of their work with cold diligence. One poem especially repelled me: a long, loving, lachrymose paean to his mother. Others of his poems were easier to take, especially those in which he wrote about the ocean and the East Hampton beach, a mile or so from his house on Montauk Highway. In his poem "Pilgrim" he writes: "The cold wind cries across the rolling dunes,/ The gray sails fleck the margins of the world."

"I lived in the City and spent weekends here in the country. I composed my poems while walking on the beach. When I'd get back to town I'd write them down. I believe I know all of my poems by heart, even the multiple versions that preceded the finished product."

The next time I met him he surprised me by saying: "Mr. Hays told me you'd borrowed some of my books. What did you think?"

I hadn't expected the question and was embarrassed that I had no answer that would circumvent my real feelings about what I disdainfully considered his out-of-date poesy.

"Don't feel bad," he interrupted my silence. "I suspect you're uneasy with the style of the poems. But you'll miss something important if you judge the past by the present. Remember what T. S. Eliot wrote? 'Some one said: "The dead writers are remote from us because we *know* so much more than they did." Precisely, and they are that which we know.'"

He went on to tell me of an experience he'd had at a Shakespeare performance. At some point he heard the line: "'Sleep on, I lie at heaven's high oriels.' I thought, God, what a wonderful line; I wish I'd written it." As it turned out, the line was not Shakespeare's at all. It was Wheelock's own creation. "Yet, I swear I heard it from the stage. That's a poet's experience, whether a poet of yesterday or today."

III. On the artist's reputation

"One generation takes the place of another, inevitably. I don't worry about how my work will be appreciated by future generations—if it is at all. My poetry is less visible than it was, and my ideas are out of favor. If I needed a mirror to reflect this, I'd contemplate my friend Van Wyck Brooks, who died some years ago. We had put together a collection of poems while at Harvard. He'd gone on to write about literature. His immense project was to read more than 800 books by American authors from the beginning of the country until our time, and to write his major work about their significance. But I see his name in the literary press infrequently these days, and I assume the public significance of his life has faded, except to his friends who still remain—to me, at least. (I remember what he said on our last visit, when he was very ill. I'd asked whether he'd like me to leave him alone. 'Oh Jack, I never want you to leave,' was his reply.) Reputation is a bubble, as is history itself."

We had been talking in the shade of the tree that transfixed the Hays' second floor porch. Although Wheelock lived around the corner, he had difficulty walking and asked if I would give him a ride home. Despite his literary accomplishments and heritage (one ancestor helped found Dartmouth college, others were fixtures of New York society), he was a modest, polite and quietly elegant man. He invited me to visit him again. "And thank you for bringing me back," he said.

44

A Feral Poet: Psychotherapy in the Hamptons

Robert was a feral poet. "That's right," he said straight-faced. "My family lives in the woods and eats berries." But I learned that was a joke: His family, though descendants of early settlers of the region, had been living in regal quietatude since the 18th century, in an ancient home on the mainland on Gardiner's Bay. What had brought them wealth, no one knew. Was it slave trading or smuggling? Not even Robert could identify the source. And, as if to make sure he didn't find out, he'd been sent to one private boarding school after another from the age of six. Each school featured some distinctively odd-ball educational philosophy—from the phantasm-dictated intuitions of Rudolf Steiner to a murderous New England boarding school with a regimen apparently based on the physical and sexual ordinances of Sparta. It was his mother's shifting philosophical whims, Robert said, that filled the sails of these crackpot educational voyages with their confusing winds.

Joking aside, I began to think that Robert might really be a bit feral, at least socially. I came to that conclusion when I considered his lack of common sense about simple things, such as how to use a knife and fork correctly, how much to tip at the Southampton diner, how extreme a favor to ask of someone, how to repay a favor done for him by someone, or how to understand someone's unexpected reaction to something he'd said. ("It was just a joke," he would tell me. "Why did the guy have to turn around and slug me?")

I offered what answers I had to his questions, but finally thought I could do something more useful for him. I'd learned that the college sponsored a local psychiatrist. Any student could book an hour of the psychiatrist's time for free. I suggested Robert make an appointment, which he did.

A couple of days later he told me what had happened. "Since they only gave me an hour, I decided to work out the best way to manage the time. I carefully psychoanalyzed myself. I felt sure I had pinpointed my various emotional crises. My hope was that the doctor could prescribe an immediate cure, since I didn't have money for psychoanalysis."

"How did it go?"

"I laid out my case as clearly as I could. He didn't say a word during that hour. After I finished he sat quietly for a few more minutes. Perhaps he was letting the clock run out? Then he said, 'You know, I think of myself as a fairly intelligent man. But I didn't understand a single thing you just told me!' Do you think I was speaking over his head?"

"Maybe," I said, trying to be diplomatic because I knew Robert's tendency to get tied up in explanations. "Or maybe next time you could go over everything piece by piece with him—break it down into little chunks," I suggested. "That way, you could help him understand what you meant."

"But I'd have to pay him for another session."

"Wouldn't your parents help you out with the money?"

"My parents? I don't talk to my parents. I don't live with them. I've forgotten their phone number!"

I was about to ask where he did live, but then remembered he'd once told me that he lived under the highway bridge at the edge of town. I was almost certain he was joking, but decided that I didn't want to know. Instead, I offered to lend him money for a psychiatric session.

The next time I saw Robert a couple of weeks later, he wanted to report how the session had gone. "You don't have to tell me anything too personal," I said.

"But I want to tell you. The psychiatrist told me we wouldn't waste our time talking, since that hadn't succeeded the first time. Instead, we'd work 'physically'. He told me he had been a student of Ida Rolfe, who invented 'deep tissue manipulation'. We'd also do some exercises invented by a doctor named Perls.

"I was to begin by stripping off my clothes and lying naked on the couch. I was then to vigorously pound on the couch with my legs while I shouted over and over: 'LEAVE ME ALONE! 'LEAVE ME ALONE!' Well, I did that for, like, a half hour. After he told me to stop, he asked me how I felt. I told him that I'd never been so frightened in my life. I felt like vomiting and going to the bathroom at the same time."

"What did he say?"

"He told me to get right up and use his bathroom before I had an accident. As I got up from the couch I saw him looking at the place where I'd been lying, I think to be sure I hadn't left anything there."

"So," I said after a moment. "This is modern psychotherapy, I suppose."

"Yes," he said. "And he wants me to come back for another session as soon as I get the money. He wants me to sit in his Orgone box to restore my energy."

I must have been looking doubtful because he rushed to tell me that he wouldn't be asking me for money to continue therapy. He'd found another source.

A couple of months passed, and Robert and I met at Guild Hall for an artist's opening. Robert took me aside to tell me how his therapy sessions had been going. From "working physically" they had moved on to more conventional talk therapy, but these sessions were enhanced by injections of various stimulant drugs, such as Ritalin. "He said if I have to talk I might as well talk for three hours straight. Maybe something would come out that would make sense for us to work on."

I told Robert that he'd got my curiosity. I'd like to meet this psychiatrist.

"Well," he said. "You can. He's standing right over there." Robert pointed to a short, stocky man in conversation with the Guild Hall's director. "It was funny." Robert said. "I was just over there. The director started to introduce me to him, but the psychiatrist told her that we already knew each other. The psychiatrist said to me, 'We know each other very well, isn't that true, Robert?'"

"What did you say?"

"I didn't know what to say."

"What were you thinking?"

"I was thinking, 'Who the hell is this guy, anyway? What right did he have saying that?'"

Despite that moment of clarity, Robert continued his therapy for a few months, funded by I never knew whom. At the last session, he told the psychiatrist his benefactor had run out of money, and would the psychiatrist care to treat him for free? The psychiatrist suggested that that might be possible if he—the psychiatrist—sold his house and went to live in a tree in the woods.

"That was sarcasm," I pointed out.

"No, I don't think so," Robert said. "I told him that I thought it was a good idea."

"What did he say?"

"He said he'd let me know. But I haven't heard from him."

And he didn't. The psychiatrist, we discovered, had given up his practice, sold his house, and moved somewhere beyond our horizon.

Robert's life, meanwhile, seemed to improve. He got a job at the village newspaper editing the police reports, which mostly logged arrests of tourist's caught urinating in public during the weekly summer traffic jams that came into town on Friday afternoons and exited Sunday nights.

Then, maybe a year after Robert's therapy ceased, he called me one night, very excited. "Turn on your TV to PBS. There's a documentary you've got to see!"

It was a documentary about the Scottish psychiatrist R. D. Laing, who maintained a kind of funny farm in the Scottish highlands where patients could live in nature, seeing if the feral life agreed with them. All sorts of people on the farm were doing odd things: talking to animals, walking like animals on all fours, hiding behind rocks, and so on. One of the inhabitants I recognized immediately. It was Robert's psychiatrist. He had stripped off his clothes and, according to the documentary's narrator, had taken to living in a tree.

"You see," Robert told me. "It wasn't sarcasm. He took my suggestion. I'd finally made sense to him!"

One of Many Random Encounters
with Truman Capote

*I'd meet Capote accidentally in obvious places: Robert Keene's book-
store in Southampton, the porch of a friend's house in Sagaponack,
up the road from where Capote lived, and various bars. Of course, I
knew who he was and what he had written. His fame awed me when
we'd first met. For his part, he seemed to remember me, but vaguely
as to my name or who or what he supposed me to be.*

I'd stopped at Bobby Van's hoping to sell the owner an advertisement in
the summer newspaper that employed me. Truman Capote was there
at a corner table. He recognized me from previous chance meetings and
lifted his arm laconically to wave me over. "You must try one of these
cocktails," he said. "You see how lovely and pink mine is, like the Sargasso
Sea? Sit down!"

I sat. "What's in it?"

"Grapefruit juice with just a little splash of vodka. I enjoy one of
these—only one—each day." He waved to the waiter. "Bring this young
man one of these."

"No thanks," I said. "I'm working today."

"Pity. Always working. Well," he said to the waiter. "You can bring me
his. Can't let this young man's drink waste away untasted."

Ilya Bolotowsky: The Bubble Reputation

*Born in 1907 in St. Petersburg, Russia, Ilya Bolotowsky was a
leading 20th-century painter in abstract styles. His work, a search
for philosophical order through visual expression, embraced cubism
and geometric abstraction and was much influenced by the Dutch
painter Piet Mondrian. He was awarded a Guggenheim Fellowship
for Creative Arts in 1973. His first solo museum show was in
1974 at New York City's Guggenheim Museum and went on to
the National Collection of Fine Arts. After teaching at the college
for many years, he moved to a studio on the Lower East Side. He
died after a fall down an elevator shaft.*

I was surprised to see Ilya Bolotowsky standing at my screen door looking
grim. As soon as he came in I noticed he wasn't alone. Revealed just
behind him were his wife, his son and his son's girlfriend. Each, one after
the other, took a seat on the couch. Each had a grim face. Sitting there,
they looked like disassembled components of a Russian nesting doll.

Bolotowsky had been my professor—English literature—an odd thing,
since he spoke with a heavy Slavic accent. But he always emphasized he was
much more than that. While primarily a painter, he was also a filmmaker,
playwright, a translator, a lecturer and an amateur airplane stunt pilot. In
his photographs, he'd be seen stroking his Cossack-type mustache, whose
wingspread measured 14½ inches. Discussing his work with interviewers
from *Art News* and *The New York Times,* he said that in his paintings "I
try for perfect harmony, using neutral elements. I want things absolutely
pure and simple. I save my feelings for my films and my plays." When I'd
asked why he pursued stunt plane flying, he said that his art dealer never
knew when he'd crash into a barn or a mountain. The uncertainty, he was
convinced, drove up the sale price of his paintings.

Bolotowsky stated his immediate business. "We've come to ask you not
to publish your story about the film we've just finished making. It will
offend my reputation."

We had spent six days shooting the film. As in most of Bolotowsky's films, the breasts of various college girls were featured, both in motion and at rest. But this film had gotten out of hand. Norman Mailer was in the middle of making his own film, *Maidstone*, in the same location, and the crews from both films intermingled. There was drinking and fighting— culminating, on Mailer's set, with the actor Rip Torn bashing Mailer's head with a hammer, and, on ours, in a late night orgy (not attended by Bolotowsky or his family, nor by me, either). However, I had thought the chaotic intertwining of the casts of both films merited a story. As a hopeful writer just graduating from college, I thought I saw an opportunity. I had not considered its effect on Bolotowsky.

He had shown me great favor by earlier designing the cover for my book of poems published by the college. He had let me direct a good part of the film we'd just made, even though my naiveté led us to chaos.

With his family staring at me, I made a quick decision and promised I wouldn't write the story.

Perhaps he sensed the fingers I had crossed behind my back. In any case, after that, he never warmed to me.

He did invite me to screen the film. I noticed that much of the provocative drunken behavior had been edited out. The nude scene that one of my friends had instigated, in which he monopolized the camera by jumping up and down shaking his penis, was now a blurred close-up of his face, which yet retained the wild grin of the manic exhibitionist.

Thinking back on this, I came to understand Bolotowsky's overwhelming need to control his reputation and his anger at me for threatening its order. He had emigrated from Russia with very little money and few prospects except his talent as a draftsman. He took the opportunities he could find and compiled them into an official biography: He was a painter and also a filmmaker, a playwright, a translator, a lecturer and an amateur airplane stunt pilot. He had a mustache with a wingspan of 14 1/2 inches. His reputation had been carefully crafted, been given life. That day, when his family, as if by his silent command, arose from my sofa, it was as if something else had risen with them, followed them back to their station wagon—something invisible, but with wings.

John MacWhinnie, A Friendship

John MacWhinnie studied painting with Willem de Kooning, Fair-field Porter, Ilya Bolotowsky and Larry Rivers. His first one man show was at Southampton College in 1966. In 1969, he had his first one man shows in New York City and his third in Southampton. His work is included in the permanent collections of the Guggenheim, Museum of Modern Art, Phillips Collection, Walker Art Center, Brooklyn, Parrish, University of Florida, and Skidmore College. His work is in private and corporate collections of the Johnson & Johnson Family, Robert Miller, Leo Castelli Estate, Willem de Kooning Estate, Fairfield Porter Estate, the Equitable Life Insurance Company, and others.

I. Thin Line

In the beginning, we found ourselves living across the street from each other on Moses Lane in Southampton. John, with his mother in their rented home, me with two roommates in another rental. One evening I came over to visit John, who was in his basement studio working at a painting. It was a wide canvas and the picture was representational—I think a landscape. When I left at about midnight he had begun painting neutral color bands on the left and right sides of the canvas, covering over some of the representational scene. By next morning, when I came over to see how he was doing, he was still working on the canvas, but now the entire picture was gone except for a narrow band of color in the center, stretching from top to bottom.

II. Geniuses

John said, "Will you take this lithograph I made for de Kooning over to his studio?" My girlfriend Susi and I drove to de Kooning's studio in the Springs. It was a building of modern design with high studio walls off the main highway. He invited us in, asked us to sit, and brought out a bottle of whiskey and a glass. "I'm not drinking anymore," he told me. "But let me pour you some of this good Scotch." He filled my glass, which must have held eight ounces, to the top. "I'll enjoy watching you drink," he said.

He sat down in a chair facing me and encouraged me to lift my glass. He said, "When I was teaching at Black Mountain College, my good friend was Buckminster Fuller, the architect. One morning I was walking past Fuller's classroom. He noticed me and called me inside. He was holding in each hand an odd piece of wood cut at complex angles. He handed the pieces of wood to me. 'I'm going to show you what a genius can do,' he told his class. He asked me to join the two pieces together so that they made a perfect fit. I turned the pieces of wood in my hands and located the most impossible angles, and the two pieces fit together perfectly! Then Fuller told us all, 'That's how a genius behaves!' But, you know," de Kooning concluded, "it was easy—nothing really. I just imagined what I would have done if I had been Fuller, and then followed the thought to its logical conclusion."

Meanwhile, Susi had been wandering around the studio looking at the paintings on easels and stacked against walls. "You enjoy your Scotch," he told me. "I'll give your friend a tour of the studio." He took Susi's arm and led her away.

I drank my Scotch. Time passed; I finished half my glass. Susi appeared, running toward me, laughing. "You'd better take me home," she said. "This guy has some ideas about what he wants to do with me."

We piled into my car and headed to John's mother's antique shop in Southampton, where John was waiting. "You know," he said. "De Kooning called my mother some time ago and told her I was a genius. That's kept me going for a long time."

III. The Blue Tree

John was thinking about what de Kooning had said when Robert Rauschenberg approached him about a conceptual art project. Rauschenberg wanted to know if de Kooning would let Rauschenberg erase one of de Kooning's drawings. De Kooning thought it over and said, "Yes, but it would have to be one of the very good drawings!"

Musing on this, John had an idea. He would ask de Kooning if he could paint one of the trees in de Kooning's yard a solid blue. The entire tree.

"So, I went to his studio," John said. "And I sat with him for a few hours trying to get the nerve to ask if I could paint the tree. It wasn't easy, and I continued to mull over how I would make my request. We talked until the sun set and, as there were no lights on in the studio, it became so dark that I could no longer see him, only hear his voice. I hadn't asked him the question, but out of the darkness he said, 'You can't paint every leaf on a tree.'

"So I went home."

IV. The Angel Natasha Visits John and Sandy

Patrizia was fed up with John, who was hard to live with. John was upset because Patrizia was no longer his Italian innocent, but a high living girl who wanted the heady Hamptons' life John had introduced to her.

John was heartbroken when Patrizia left. But then the Angel Natasha, daughter of a famous Russian pianist, a pianist herself and a singer appeared to him. She offered to console him, to sing for him. But he was too desolated to accept her offer.

Meanwhile, I was playing the piano in one of the practice rooms behind the Fine Arts Theater stage. Many of us played at night, sometimes competing with each other, sometimes gently serenading. Oddly, no one ever introduced themselves; at evening's end we left without anyone seeing us.

However, one night, when I was playing a Chopin mazurka I especially liked, and was tearful because of the great love it evoked, the Angel

Natasha appeared to me. She burst into the room and shouted: "Will you kindly stop murdering that Chopin mazurka? Let me show you how it should be played." But I packed up my music and left the room, too desolated to accept her offer.

V. Natal Chart

John and I discovered we'd been born in the same town, seventy miles from the Hamptons, in the same hospital, in the same small maternity building, two years apart. If it can't be proved that we were born in the same bed, it is known that from birth on we howled like banshees.

Robert Bly's Light and Sound

At this time, the Hamptons were considered remote. Distances from major cities seemed greater. Television broadcasts we could get originated from a couple of Connecticut stations across the Sound, blurred, diving and swimming through the swells. Even so, my poet teachers and friends were aware of a persistent voice reaching us from far-off Minnesota, broadcasting its ideas and dicta clearly, forcefully—sometimes outrageously. The voice was Robert Bly's.

We read Bly's striking polemics in his own magazines, *The Sixties* and *The Seventies*. His anti-war activities also made the news, as did his winning of the National Book Award for his collection, *The Light Around the Body*. He made a speech at the award ceremony that produced the kind of headlines poets rarely see.

He also exerted a pull on H.R. Hays and David Ignatow. Bly and James Wright had discovered Latin American poetry in Hays' earlier pioneering translations. In his introduction to Hays' *Selected Poems 1933–67*, Wright wrote: "... Hays begins and remains one of the finest American poets precisely because he has been able to absorb into our language and into our life the immense poetry that exists among people who hate us, who frighten us, who fight us, who can teach us, and who love us.... To discover his own poems is only to confirm what I had felt about his love of the [Latin American] masters."

Bly had also written about what he believed to be the important aspects of David Ignatow's poetry. After Ignatow's *Selected Poems* was issued in 1970, Bly convinced him that we (those of us who helped Ignatow with his original editing) just didn't get where Ignatow was coming from. Bly demanded to edit the next edition himself.

I walked through the second floor sliding glass doorway of the Hays' home in the East Hampton woods carrying a stack of a *kayak* poetry magazines. Hoffman and Julie had encouraged me to drop in any time I was in the neighborhood, but now I saw that I was interrupting something. Sitting with them at the dining table was a big man glowering at me.

"You see what he's been reading, George?" Hays said to the man, indicating the stack of magazines under my arm. "Sandy, I'd like you to meet George Hitchcock. He's the editor of *kayak.*"

Of course, I recognized his name. He'd already rejected three of my poetry submissions, each rejection letter featuring an appropriately gruesome Victorian image or collage. On the one hand, these were hilarious; on the other, they were a direct challenge. I'd taped them to my bathroom wall, along with other less spectacular rejections I'd begun to receive. Meeting Hitchcock at that moment cowed me. I mumbled my greetings, placed the stack of *kayaks* on the coffee table, and withdrew. I was nineteen, and George Hitchcock was, in my secret thoughts, a literary star—in the Hollywood sense of the word—the first I'd met outside of the Hamptons' archipelago.

kayak was an exciting magazine, both form and content. It seemed to have been printed on whatever paper was lying around. In fact, the Contents page of *kayak* 19 declares:

> NOTICE: The major portion of this issue of *kayak* has been printed on rifle and small-arms target paper rejected as substandard by the U.S. Defense Department

The magazine, like its rejection letters, featured illustrations from Victorian books and magazines, some of which Hitchcock had collaged. The magazine covers, as well as the covers of poetry collections he printed, were illustrated with these, too. Sometimes the result was quite lovely; at other times, not so. But it was the content that was exciting.

I'd been reading poems in the *Hudson, Sewanee, Kenyon* and other establishment poetry reviews available at the college library. I was also familiar with the burgeoning genre of little magazines, such as *Cloud Marauder* and *lillibulero,* that Hays and Ignatow published in. But the most exciting discoveries I'd made, such as the poems of James Tate and Charles Simic, had been published in *kayak.* I was determined that *kayak* would publish me, too.

kayak published deep imagist and neo-Surrealist poems and, for all I could see, rejected the kind of stodgy stuff published in the *Hudson Review*. In fact, its writers went further, and attacked the establishment magazines. In this way, a national community of "*kayak*" poets had been created.

By the twelfth issue, Hitchcock apparently decided to shake things up a bit. He asked Robert Bly to write an article, "The First Ten Issues of *kayak*." Bly begins: "George Hitchcock asked me for some prose for *kayak*, and I asked if I might do an attack on his first ten issues. He thought that was a good idea."

Preparing the ground (i.e. setting up his defenses) for what is to come, he suggests that "some people feel that criticism is always destructive, like an overexposure to X-rays." He says that this impression comes from the 'fifties, when Robert Lowell, Karl Shapiro and their generation were the dominant critics, but not good ones. "They were always looking up into the sky: who was there? Yeats.... His solitary rocket-like career was the only model." Consequently, writers were out for themselves. In reaction to this, Bly asserts, the Black Mountain poets formed a kind of mutual protective society with their criticism, making loyalty to the "Olson creed" a virtue.

> These two approaches to criticism, capitalistic dog-eat-dog competitiveness and corporative 'don't knock the company' team-spirit, both seemed good ideas at the time, but both approaches now seem big failures. There is a third possibility: those who are interested in the same sort of poetry attack each other sharply, and still have respect and affection for each other.... The criticism of my own poetry that has been the most use to me has been criticism that, when I first heard it, utterly dismayed me.

Bly, having assured us of his respect and affection, now casts himself in the role of the kindly physician, who asks us to drop our pants and bend over as he flourishes the silver syringe. "This will only hurt for a moment. It's good for you," he seems to say.

"I think the first ten issues have been on the whole clogged and bad. As an editor, George Hitchcock is too permissive.... Too much foggy stuff gets in: in *kayak* poems usually someone is stepping into a tunnel of dark wind and disappearing into a whistle: the darkness is always pausing to wait for someone."

He diagrams the typical *kayak* image:

> ... they are made of a) an animal or object, b) a violent action, c) an adjective (often *tiny, dark* or *great*), and then d) the geographical location. "Lighted cigars fall like meteors on a deserted football field in Pierre, South Dakota."

He goes after the faults of certain poets specifically: an example of "crystallized flower formations from the jolly intellectual dandies" (Richard Wilbur), and "the high-pitched bat-like cry of the anal Puritan mandarin" (Gilbert Sorrentino).

kayak poets write about "trees, leaves, animals, plants, nature poems." The big problem with the typical *kayak* poem is that it seems always to have been written at the poet's desk, and not out in the field. He quotes Bashō: "To express the flavor of the inner mind, you must agonize during many days." "The Japanese say, 'Go to the pine if you want to learn about the pine'." If American poets wants to write about, for instance, "a chill and foggy field," they have to stay out there, and get cold and wet themselves. He concludes with an instruction both outrageous and unforgettable (at least for me): "Two hours of solitude seem about right for every line of poetry."

In the "Letters" section of the next issue, George Hitchcock writes: "Robert Bly's review ... has provoked an unprecedented amount of comment." He then prints excerpts from nine letters addressing the review. Some, written by those directly or inferentially attacked by Bly, launched counter-attacks. Morton Marcus begins his:

> Captain Bly has been on a rampage once again, flogging the innocent, seeking the elusive Christian he loves but is bent on destroying, and shouting orders which few of us can understand. As often happens with the good skipper, his trusty astrolabe enables him to find the right direction, but somehow he misses port by several thousand miles.

Richard Wilbur, one of the two poets actually named and castigated by Bly responds personally:

> Having extolled a campy magazine
> As a "fist" raised against my kind of writing,
> What will you tell me know, friend? That you mean
> No harm, of course, and would not dream of fighting.
> And have but put, in furtherance of your Mission,
> A little punch into your disquisition.
> Granted that it's a figurative fist;
> That critics punch as harmlessly as kittens,
> That you have merely slapped me on the wrist
> With one of *kayak's* puce Alaskan mittens;
> Nevertheless, when you incite to riot
> Against your friend, he is not pleasured by it.

Several other letters, including a long one from John Haines (whom Bly specifically exempts from his criticism) make the suggestion that, though Bly seems to be pointing his finger squarely at the faults of others, in fact, his complaints are as true about his own poetry as about anyone's.

The appearance of Bly's critique caused an excitement among the Hamptons poets, especially Hays and Ignatow, who had published in the magazine. Hays faulted Bly for his accusation that Hitchcock published his magazine quarterly and that that "hectic" schedule caused him to publish a lot of stuff that might not get into a magazine appearing less frequently. "If you only get around to publishing an issue every other year," Hays writes, comparing Hitchcock's output to Bly's own magazine publishing, "you never rid yourself of the taint of dilettantism, something Bly has never shed." Hays then adds something that I think is revealing of his moral [ethical?] point of view, typical of his time in which printing and distributing a poetry magazine were not such easy things: "Something has to be *kept going.*"

After four decades, I recall the furor Bly's critique stirred up at the time of publication, but after re-reading it, as well as the poems, he criticizes, I find the furor difficult to understand. On re-reading I was disappointed that the review was not as ruthless and bloody as I'd recalled it. And, to my surprise, some of the *kayak* poems Bly holds up to scorn are indeed terrible. Here, Louis Hammer cobbles together some *kayak* images:

> Pirates have nailed the hands of neurosurgeons
> To the masts of ships crushed by Charlemagne's armies;
> ...
> Aaron Burr paddles down the Hudson
> In a jeweled kayak bearing Hamilton's liver.
> The Republic waves silk flags at the finish line.

Granted, he's using these lines ironically, as his concluding stanza makes clear:

> Mao Tse Tung washes the scales from [Lorca's horse's]
>   back.
> He intones: "Two hours of fraternizing
> For every line of a revolutionary poem."

I found that many of the poems that had baffled and intrigued me when I was in my teens now leave me scratching my head. (Of course, this is not fair of me and I should abide by Eliot's cautionary on looking at the past, and at the meaning of Butterfield's title, *The Whig Interpretation of History*, in which the temptation to look over one's shoulder at the past is really looking at history through the wrong end of the telescope.) But in any case, two conclusions remain: First, that Bly was correct when he wrote: "At the same time *kayak* is valuable, and a much-loved magazine. Unlike the *Kenyon Review*, which everyone for years has been hoping would kick off soon, *kayak* would be missed very much if it developed a leak and sank..."

It is this love for the magazine and the community it encouraged that brought its poets out to mount a defense. They were not really defending the poetry, but rather the community itself. I know that *kayak*'s neo-surrealism was just what I needed to get started with my own poetry. Had I been born twenty years before, I would not have been happy with the poetic and critical world I would have found. I think others were glad of it, too.

Second, I think Bly was at least one step ahead of us *kayak* readers. I think he knew, master debater that he was, exactly what he was doing. As well as—or probably much more than—wanting to help out critically he wanted to stir things up, to make a loud noise with the purpose of keeping his name in lights.

He'd gamed us.

Tunneling Into the Next Life:
Three Hamptons Poets and Their Final Work

David Ignatow died in November 1997. Armand Schwerner died in February 1999. Harvey Shapiro died in 2014. Posthumous poetry collections by Ignatow, Schwerner and Shapiro were published within a year following their deaths. In the case of Schwerner's poetry, two collections were brought out—a complete set of his well-known *Tablets*, including a CD of their live performance, and a volume of his lesser-known shorter poems. In the case of Ignatow's poetry, a collection of last poems was notably edited by three people who were close to him: his daughter, Yaedi, Virginia Terris, and Jeannette Hopkins, who long-ago shaped some of the seminal collections of his work originally published by Wesleyan University Press. Shapiro's poetry was gathered by his friend and literary executor, Norman Finkelstein. The book was published by Wesleyan.

Ignatow and Schwerner shared little of poetic method. Their cultural and religious backgrounds were similar—both grew up in New York City and both credited Walt Whitman as their literary forbear—but Schwerner was a poet who rejoiced in an abundance, often a manic torrent of language, while Ignatow pared his words frugally. Yet, in the company of other poets, painters, photographers, filmmakers and sculptors who spent summers together in the wooded community of East Hampton known as the Springs from the late-1960's, these two became great friends.

Armand Schwerner

Armand and his family lived in a small house off Fireplace Road. Armand's wife, Dolores, was an artist whose work anticipated Performance art. Their two boys, Ari and Adam were blond like their mother but had their father's exuberant personality. When I first visited their home Ari, who was six, and Adam, who was eight, delighted in scandalizing me with a nursery rhyme written by their father, which begins:

One room of the grey rat
two room for the cowlick
seven room for moose
and Muck the Fuck to celebrate;

...

Room for the real.
Kitchen of shadows, bing.
If you don't sing
what's out there?

("Muck the Fuck")

Armand, aware that I was made uncomfortable by such things, made a point of instructing me in his version of a less WASPish life. Among several of his lessons I recall arriving home with him one late night and watching him demonstrate what he declared in his booming voice to be the best part of capitalism: the freedom to piss all over your own front lawn.

At the time Armand had published a small collection of poetry, *The Lightfall*. Mark Weiss' Junction Press, publisher of his *Selected Shorter Poems*, has included six of the best from this rare, early book. It is usually a mistake to look backwards at a series of poems and point out how they presaged a poet's later writing interests. However, in these six representative poems one can find the poetic approaches and methods that occupied Armand's attention throughout much of his life. A poem like "where the boat passes, improvise," with lines such as "he sits with Stone the Death/ and munches by the Door// will he eat papyrus in the drummer's hallway?" sounds right out of his later *Tablets*; in "the Other" lines such as "we are two bodies, a comb,/ hatband, brush, a mouth moving" suggest his later meditations of *Sounds of the River Naranjana...*; and so on. Of this first volume, only "the red horses of the sun" represents a kind of formality I don't believe he ever sought again: "red is the color of spring/ it feeds that pattern of her flesh// it stutters in its course under the rare earth"—a poet's student work.

Despite the great critical attention given to *The Tablets* as each volume was published, I think some of Schwerner's best poetic urges were realized in the often hilarious and above all, loving poems inspired by his children and by that part of him that was childlike. Wonderful examples of these—such as "Muck the Fuck," "Poem at the bathroom door, by Adam," and "What Ari says when he's five"—are reprinted from his first two books. In his third book, he again realizes these antic urges, this time in his translation of Eskimo poems. This infectious humor, I think, has been Schwerner's saving grace (at least for lyric pleasure-seekers like me), for as he continued to write he became preoccupied with weightier subjects that he believed he must present with due, unsmiling seriousness. I'm not convinced that his rendering of Buddhist themes, for example, shows a lessening of his personal self-importance, of his intrusive presence in the poems—rather the opposite. However, despite this, these poems show him to be a poet of dedication and great, if naïve, ability—his naiveté demonstrated by the partial title of one book, *The Triumph of the Will*. (When I asked him didn't he know that this had been the title of Leni Riefenstahl's infamous 1935 Nazi propaganda film, Armand protested that he had never heard of it.)

Although Junction Press' edition of Armand's *Selected Shorter Poems* does not include some of my favorites, it does feature some of his most moving. We happened to be together in the Springs when David Ignatow gave us the news that Paul Blackburn had died. One of us—probably H.R. Hays—organized a memorial reading for Paul at the Old Post Office Theater in East Hampton. Armand's poem was especially poignant. Its title describes it well: "a letter to Paul Blackburn preceded by a letter Rainer Maria Rilke wrote 13 days before his death in 1826 to Rudolph Kassner." The poignancy of these lines continues fresh, and could serve as Armand's own epitaph.

a letter to Paul Blackburn preceded by a letter Rainer Maria Rilke wrote 13 days before his death in 1926 to Rudolph Kassner

my dear Kassner, so this it was
of which my nature has been urgently forewarning me
for three years: I am ill
in a miserable and infinitely
painful way, a little-known cell alteration in the blood
is becoming the point
of departure
for the most horrible occurrences
scattered through my entire body. And I,
who never wanted to look it squarely in the face
am learning to adjust myself
to the incommensurable
anonymous
pain. Am learning it with difficulty,
amid a hundred resistances,
and so sadly amazed. I wanted you to know of this
condition of mine
which will not be of the most passing. Inform the dear
    Princess of it,
as much as you consider well

my dear Paul, so this it is
that I never wanted to look at squarely in the face
you are ill
in a miserable way that Jerry and Si and Joany say
is not infinitely painful, a well-known cell alteration in
    the epithelium
becomes the point
of departure
for the most horrible occurrences

scattered through your entire body. And I,
who never wanted to look it squarely in the face
will be working for the rest of my life to adjust myself
to the incommensurable
anonymous
pain. Am learning it with difficulty,
amid a hundred resistances,
and so sadly amazed. I wanted you to know of this
    condition of mine
which will not be of the most passing, that your passing is
into us, bodies and poems, Paul dear, is very little comfort
    to you but it is
what there is for both you and us.

Sections of *The Tablets* have appeared in several volumes over the years, but it is the present collection that includes all twenty seven of them, along with copious notes and appendices. *The Tablets* are Schwerner's best known work, mainly because he promoted them in a great number of live perfor-mances (at which he was expert—an accompanying CD attests to this) and in print. Consequently, they have and continue to receive a good deal of critical attention. They represent supposed remnants of Sumero-Akka-dian clay tablets as interpreted by Armand's alter-ego, the "Scholar-Trans-lator." Those who have heard Armand read them have knowledge of the poet as a performer—a genuine stage performer whose material demanded that he give his Tablets much more bravura than a poet's usual reading— something Hays characterized as "the poet mumbling into his beard." The Tablets embody the full range of Armand's poetic power, as well as his great strengths and fallibilities as a person, as well. Thus, the Scholar-Translator begins as a figure of fun—a pompous academic bumbling through his mis-interpretations of the meaning of his translations—but later changes into an ironic, if unsmiling authority—a man demanding, as Armand seemed to demand at the end, that people take him seriously.

Armand was often as delightful a companion as his friends found him difficult to abide. In his later years, his incessant preoccupation with himself was only made tolerable by his ever-sharpening, ever-darker, explosive wit. During the last years of his life, Armand and I saw little of each other. Part of this is because, following his divorce from Dolores (who owned the Springs house), Armand no longer had a base on Long Island. But much of our alienation had to do with our competing Buddhist philosophies. Even after his guru was exposed as a drunk and lecher—and mine as a womanizing thief—we rarely saw each other. I think we spoke only once or twice in his last two years. I had published an account of my Buddhist experience in *Tricycle* magazine to which he subscribed. He called to let me know how delighted he was to discover that I had made him a character in the story, identified as "A." I was thrilled to hear from him, and had indeed written him into the story, hoping it would break the ice between us. Our conversation that time embodied the warmth that had been missing between us for years.

David Ignatow

Reading again this final collection of David Ignatow's poetry many years after his death is a wonderful surprise. There he is, speaking again, not in the tired voice of an opera singer who has made one-too-many farewell appearances, but in his steadfast, forceful voice, with its inimitable preoccupations and ironies. At first the voice is quiet, abstract: "Fear is of the universe,/as is death,/ as is love, pleasure,/ intimacy and cruelty." But then it picks up its familiar sonority: "Interesting that I have to live with my skeleton./ It stands, prepared to emerge, and I carry it/ with me—this other thing I will become at death."

In the first section of poems in this book I visualize Ignatow coming to the screen door of his study, answering my tentative knock, his voice, thinner in his last years, and his movements slower, but his eyes demanding directness and honesty. I've told the story elsewhere about my early experience with him when, after I'd bragged of reading an unbelievably large number of books during a short period of time, Ignatow reacted as if truly hurt by my exaggeration. "You must use language responsibly," he admonished me then. This directness is mirrored in the sobriety of these poems.

David, like Armand, could frustrate his friends by his obtrusive self-involvement. Harvey Shapiro told the story of how one day David telephoned to announce "I've got wonderful news for you, Harvey!" Since Harvey was then in contention for an important poetry prize that David might know about he was thrilled by David's call. However, it proved to be disappointing when David revealed that the "wonderful news" was, of course, about David, not Harvey. It probably never occurred to David that Harvey would be expecting to hear something else.

While their approach to writing differed greatly, Armand and David shared preoccupations in common, notably with personal mortality. Between David's and Armand's rendering of this theme, I believe David had the advantage, since his poetic postmortem was not burdened with the formality of some *a priori* philosophy or religion—whereas Armand's was. The "last poems" in Ignatow's collection testify to his unblinking examination of his own mortality that he began in *Shadowing the Ground* several years earlier. Armand's "last poems" (which I suppose to be those recent ones in his *Selected* collection under the heading "uncollected"), while passionate and intellectually rigorous, still carry the unopened baggage of religious aspiration: "but this blood, which transforms/ the five poisons into the five knowledges, this blood/ of great passion, passionless, free of passion,/ this secret great blood, free of clinging…" ("blood"). These images are specifically Buddhist shorthand; readers not familiar with them may enjoy their exotic mystery but are not helped to face, along with the poet, the reality of Death Itself. In terms of a winning strategy, I give the laurels to Ignatow:

> What I thought I was writing—
> for the social good—turns out to be
> for my own enlightenment;
> no one is listening.
>
> ("How I learned to be with others")

Harvey Shapiro

After Ignatow's final book was published, Robert Bly wrote that Ignatow had done what very few writers have done: continue to advance their poetry, their eyes open and alert, to tell the rest of us of their journey through old age and death. In *A Momentary Glory*, I think Harvey has taken Ignatow's lead. The poems in this collection represent a sustained effort to report on the journey, now that the quotidian worries of earlier times— when we still suspected we might live forever—are no longer as pertinent as they once were. Poetry concerning one's end, recited in tears, would be excruciating. Happily, this does not describe the last poems of Ignatow and Shapiro, who pick up the challenge with enthusiasm. Ignatow writes:

> Am I complaining of the shortness of life?
> I am, and that makes me much like everyone else.
> Follow Adam, the leader, into the ground.
> (Where I built my house)

And Harvey joins in:

> In my final years
> I have moved into a basement apartment
> so I can get used to the steps
> of the living above me
> and to their sweet weight.
> (Planning)

A certain amount of farting initiates the old age poems of Ignatow and Shapiro. Ignatow writes: "Old men spend their days farting/ in private to entertain themselves/ in the absence of friends/ long since gone." Shapiro, taking a public stance, writes: "Let's go out/ and fart in the sunlight." (I don't have a theory about this; I only wish that Robert Bly, with his Sousaphone voice, were here to inform us of the governing mythos....)

While Armand and David taught for a living, Harvey, who began as a teacher, went into journalism. He was an editor with *The New York*

Times from 1957 until his retirement in 1995. At *The Times* he edited *The Times Magazine* and *The Times Book Review*, a post he held from 1975 to 1983. In the early 1960s, as an editor at *The Times Magazine*, Harvey made what was almost certainly his most inspired journalistic assignment. Reading about one of Dr. King's frequent jailings, he contacted the Southern Christian Leadership Conference. Harvey suggested to them that the next time Dr. King was in jail for any significant period he should compose a letter for publication, the setting alone would demand wide attention. This came about: Dr. King was jailed in Birmingham and wrote what has come to be known as his *Letter From Birmingham Jail*, one of the canonical texts of the civil rights movement. King had it delivered to Harvey at *The Times*, but, after much effort, Harvey failed to get his editors to run it. It was famously published elsewhere—a sign of those times (and, then, of *The New York Times*).

I'm not sure I can pinpoint how Harvey's work affected his poetry—or how David's or Armand's affected theirs. But I'm mindful of Tomas Tranströmer's insight, "With his work, as through a glove, a man feels the universe," and know that the relationship between our outer and inner lives is delineated there.

Norman Finkelstein has arranged these poems in an order that I think reflects Harvey's wishes, since he knew that this book would be summative. Harvey's method in these poems is to dip into his subjects as if into a well, and to taste just what the ladle brings up. He reaches for his poetic forebears: In Williams he discovers that "The bread of life is what we die to taste./ I taste it in your poems." Reznikoff was after a Chinese clarity. "He said/ two things Oppen, Louis, Rakosi and he/ had in common: they couldn't get published/ and they admired the Do's and Don'ts/ Ezra Pound was publishing in *Poetry*." Oppen, rejecting a crucifix waived over his head on a battlefield by a concerned Catholic chaplain, was a man "who called things by their right names" when he protested that the cross was an instrument of torture.

As with others of Harvey books, there's a certain amount raffish of sex here. Finkelstein suggests that Harvey is one of our great erotic poets. I would say Harvey had a lot of fun in this realm and I'd rather characterize

him as just plain (or even elegantly) horny. He gives us some lovely rec-
ollections of past lovers, and also a hilarious consideration of King Kong:

> You never actually see it in the movie.
> When he's ... batting at planes.... [But] when
> he's got Fay Wray in the palm
> of his hand, you know it's reaching
> gigantic proportions,
> but below the screen.
>
> (King Kong's Wong)

As he has all his life, he writes of Brooklyn and Manhattan. He includes
other places: Key West, and Europe, beginning in Paris and ending at Franz
Kafka's grave in Prague. But his starting and ending point is Brooklyn. In
"Psalm" he is alone on a Brooklyn rooftop considering Rabbi Nachman's
description of the world as a narrow bridge "and that the important thing/
is not to be afraid." He blesses his mother and father, and asks that

> before you close your Book of Life ...
> remember that I always praised your word
> and your splendor and that my tongue
> tried to say your name on Court Street in Brooklyn.

Always, as a young soldier assembling a machine gun blindfolded, or an
older man assembling a poem in the same way, Harvey works, as he de-
scribes Mozart working: turning and returning, "that some basic law, like
gravity,/ is constantly defied."

His Best Friends Buried There

Green River Cemetery has been expanded by at least an acre or two behind Pollock's boulder. Artists and writers continue to be buried there, and who they were and what they are famous for reflects something of the upscale attraction of the modern Hamptons. Filmmakers such as Stan Vanderbeek and producer Alan Pakula are buried there, as is the celebrated French chef, Pierre Franey, to name three. [*For a casual list of others buried there see* Notes]The cost of graves, I understand, is prohibitively expensive, except for the very wealthy—as is everything else thereabouts. Even so, the cemetery was silent countryside at my last visit as all of the Springs had once been, even at the height of summer. I reflected on my encounter with de Kooning years before, and had the sobering thought that in subsequent summers a tipsy artist wobbling on his bicycle on a Hampton's road would have little chance of surviving the tourist traffic, which is grim, relentless and unforgiving. In fact, I realized that the easy access I had in my time to the wonderful artists and writers living there may no longer be possible. These days they all seem to remain cloistered in their compounds, their public appearances protected by bodyguards.

At Canio's bookstore in Sag Harbor some years ago, Harvey Shapiro read a poem called "For Armand and David" that touched on feelings shared by those of us who have considered the Hamptons a refuge for our poetic selves.

"When we were young," Shapiro begins:

> And our children were young—
> the water was such a mystery,
> the sky so blue. Everything
> breathed promise. The language
> would blaze forth,
> did blaze forth…

To the rich vacationers
our lives meant nothing.
We kept investing them with meaning
until the enterprise broke us.

…

I see these same sights,
bleared now. Words
broken into stony syllables,
blackened in remembrance.

At the end of 1970—and as we did each year back then—Armand, David, Harvey, Hoffman Hays, Allen Planz, Si Perchick, R. B. Weber, and others of us gathered during November or December to celebrate some last event before winter. A few times I remember Armand grunting a kind of benediction to end the season. "And now," he'd pronounce in his ominous tones, "for four months of shit."

We'd look up into the grey sky, and that would be it till we'd meet again in spring.

QUESTIONS AFTER A HISTORY:
A RECAPITULATION

*The facts are really not at all like fish on the fishmonger's slab.
They are like fish swimming about in a vast and sometimes in-
accessible ocean; and what the historian catches will depend, ...
mainly on what part of the ocean he chooses to fish in.*

—E. H. CARR, *What Is History?*

The Plagiarist's Heart

Sidney S., the screenwriter, on how he became a writer:

In high school I was too lazy, or I ran out of time—or for some other reason I borrowed my roommate's A+ English paper and copied my name to it. I have to say it was impressively written. But I didn't expect my English teacher to give it an F and drag me to the principal's office.

"This young man," Mr. McGowan told the principal in a drooling frenzy: "I've caught him cheating—cheating again! This time he stole an article from *The New York Times Book Review* I'm sure! This time he must be suspended from school!"

The principal wasn't ready to follow through (my father, after all, a big donor). "Let's test him," said the principal. "Give him another writing assignment and see if it reaches the quality of this one."

I knew my English teacher would rather have kicked me, punched me, battered me. He was one of those violent English teachers, a wrestling coach, loved to spank his class' wise-guys with a dictionary. But he sat me down in the empty classroom and ordered a writing assignment.

He gave me thirty minutes to write about something—I forget what. For a while I was lost, had no idea how to do it. Then I thought about the paper I'd plagiarized. I thought about its organization: the strong, clear first sentence. Supportive sentences to follow. Then the unfurling of ideas into separate first second third fourth fifth paragraphs. Finally, a big idea to gather all the smaller ones together. Of course, you'll say, this is nothing but classical rhetoric. But at that moment, untutored, I was discovering something for myself. An embracing vision. It had the land, the mountains and the sky in it. I could breathe its air!

I organized my thoughts, then, and wrote.

At the end of thirty minutes, my teacher snatched the paper. He was going to get me this time!

He devoured it—there's no other word to describe his hunger. I watched as he read, his face intent, but then, falling, as if it were a wall of attenuating brick and mortar. Finally, he told me I could go.

That was the last I heard from him or anyone. I was no longer an F student. And I knew then, without doubt, that I would be a writer.

Hemingway Completes His Introduction to
A Moveable Feast

"This book is fiction. I have left out much and changed and elimi-
nated and I hope Hadley understands. She will see why I hope. She
is the heroine and the only person who had a life that turned out
well and as it should except certain of the rich."

—ERNEST HEMINGWAY. One of twelve false starts on his
Introduction. (Item 122. The Hemingway Collection.
John F. Kennedy library, Boston.)

There is cleanliness to those years in Paris which is not fiction, and
harmony and logical order that I did not notice when I was living and
inventing it, though it seems obvious and self-evident now. We were in
love and innocent, and, in the end, produced a lovely, innocent child by
the name of Mr. Bumby, who should have had us by his side more years
than he did. Few of us were aware of the dark drawstrings of personality.
I taught Ezra to box, and we enjoyed joking about the Jews, which was
all harmless at the time. If Joyce or Miss Stein noticed the shadow of my
father's shotgun clamped in my jaws, that I rattled and shook at them to
make a point, they never mentioned it. And it would not have been out
of politeness or modesty, as neither was modest, though both were direct
and often polite.

This book is fiction, but it is also true. Hadley and I were poor in
Paris, but simple and honest, because of it. Only in the end, when there
was a little money and late mountain nights and skiing and dinners and
drink under the lanterns, when our attentions turned from each other to
newer faces and adventures, did we lose our way.

Hadley is the heroine, her image bright above the lanterns of wom-
en and cities. Hadley is the light that led me, in the end, to this white
room in Ketchum of which the tourists will ask. "Why this room? Why
so small?" I would answer: *Poverty and innocence live in small rooms, and*

the room Hadley and I share grows smaller in my eyes as I sit in this chair, my father's shotgun—anonymous steel—clamped in my jaws, as I prepare at length to address that issue.

A Curious Case:
Dr. Irvin D. Yalom Treats Bartleby the Scrivener

for George Whitson

I had not wanted to treat Bartleby, but a fan of my accounts of my ther-
apeutic experiences with patients wrote to urge me on. He questioned
my use of literary techniques to shape the stories I tell in my books and
suggested that by using the discourse of fiction I was unfairly spotlighting
the power of my curative insights. While I have always held that my lit-
erary style is intended to sharpen the focus of my narrative, not obscure
it, my fan expressed his doubts. "Doctor," he wrote. "Isn't it time that
you, a non-fictional literary character, confront Bartelby, an undoubtedly
fictional one who needs the help only a therapist of your literary mastery
can provide?"

Of course, I was flattered by his praise, but disconcerted by his ref-
erence to me as a "non-fictional literary character," although to him,
whom I have never met, I remain a character on the printed page only.
In any case, among the many fictional characters in need of professional
help, Bartleby was an excellent candidate, so I decided to give it a shot.

I knew from reading Melville's story that Bartleby is hired as a law
clerk in a nineteenth century lawyer's office on Wall Street. At first, he
does his job—copying legal writs and briefs—to the great satisfaction
of his employer. However, after some months, he begins to neglect his
work, instead sitting at his desk, staring into space. When his employer
demands that he explain his obduracy he refuses, replying simply that "I
prefer not to." From then on, these words become his refusal to all calls
to action, until his story takes him to an extremely remote, uncommuni-
cative end—in fact, silence and death in a prison cell.

Intrigued, I put out word that I was interested in him, and soon got a
reply. That Bartleby kept our appointment at all was remarkable. He en-
tered my office, a tall man, slightly bent, as men and women who are tall
and wish they weren't often bend to disguise it. In any case, he looked

exactly as I'd imagined him—not surprising since I was, in fact, just then imagining him. He sat on my sofa without a word and looked at me, waiting for me to speak.

I began the consultation asking about any problem he might have. When that didn't elicit a response, I asked about his work, his family, his social life, and so on, but without success. Not a word! As I continued to question him I noticed that his lips twitched involuntarily, as if trying to smile. Finally, by the end of our session, I found him grinning broadly without once having answered a question, as if he were conscious of the tremendous power his inaction might be having over other people's lives—my life, in point of fact.

I rose from my chair and told him gently that our time was up. Bartleby, however, remained seated. After waiting for his reaction I repeated firmly that our hour was up and he must go.

Then he spoke for the first time. "I prefer not to," said he.

I explained that I had other patients waiting, but Bartleby didn't move. Finally I gave up and left the room. For the rest of the day I saw my patients in the reception area—specifically in the tight confines of the reception hall closet—to insure confidentiality.

The next day, with some trepidation, I opened my office door. Bartleby was there, seated on the couch as I had left him the day before. I cannot say that he was waiting for me; he paid no attention when I spoke to him. I told him that he must leave the office. Didn't he have a job to go to? Wasn't that important to him?

"I prefer not to," said he.

All at once I had a vision of how this would end. Instead of dying of malnutrition in jail, since he preferred not to eat, Bartleby would die of malnutrition in my office. This would be terrible! The university would have to remove the man by police ambulance. There would certainly be an uproar on campus. I would not only have to admit that I had failed in Bartleby's case, but admit it publically! This tug of war between my non-fiction discourse and my fiction discourse had indeed ended badly.

But, as invariably happens in the case narratives I write, I was able to turn the situation to advantage. One afternoon, when returning to my office from lunch, I met a young patient coming out of my door. Suddenly apprehensive, I asked her if she had noticed the man sitting on the sofa. "He's your student, right?" she asked.

Since I occasionally allow my advanced students to hold sessions with patients, I recognized her misunderstanding. "Did the man on the couch say anything to you?" I asked.

"No, he didn't. But he has a wonderful way of listening. Very calming."

"He's a Freudian, of course," I improvised to explain his silence.

"Well, I enjoyed our session. I felt I could tell him anything!"

After that, as an experiment, I encouraged others of my patients to visit "Dr. Bartleby." Their reactions were identical, all positive and admiring. In fact, his popularity as a therapist increased to the degree that I thought I had better end his "professional" career sooner, rather than later, if I were to keep my own following.

With his case closed, I learned eventually to stop thinking about him—at which point, of course, Bartleby disappeared.

And, while my copy of *Bartleby the Scrivener* collects dust in my bookshelf, the face of Bartleby does show up occasionally in my imaginings, of late transplanted onto Edgar Allen Poe's, "The Raven."

> And Bartleby, never flitting, still is sitting, still is sitting
> On the psychiatric sofa just inside my chamber door...

Goethe Writes *Aus meinem Leben:*
Dichtung und Wahrheit (1811–1833)

Goethe's friends are entreating him to write the autobiography. One friend says: "We try to guess many a riddle, to solve many a problem." But soon they've reached an impasse. His friends beg him: "You might give us a little assistance now and then, here and there. Would you?"

"Their desire," Goethe writes, "so kindly expressed, immediately awakened within me an inclination to comply. But how? One cannot simply write everything that has happened. One needs method. It must be a very agreeable and a re-animating task to treat former creations as new matter, and work them up into a kind of Last Part." He realizes he cannot include everything, so he selects incidents, compresses or expands others, eliminates many.

He feels the danger, diddling with history, but he has an honest end to achieve. He declares the title of his autobiography: *Dichtung und Wahrheit, Poetry and Truth*.

Immediately, it is misconstrued in the press. *Dichtung* is understood as meaning Fiction. "What has Goethe given us?" they ask. "Is it part fiction, part truth? And indeed, which part is which?"

"No, no, no!" Goethe screams. [I translate freely here.] "It was my endeavor to present and express to the best of my ability the actual basic truths that controlled my life as I understood them." The work is translated into English as *Lies and Truth in My Life*. "Scheiße Kopf!" shrieks Goethe [in my free translation].

"Lies? Are they all idiots? I wanted the word *Dichtung* understood not in the sense of fabrication but as the revelation of higher truths. Doesn't anyone see this?"

"They say your novel, *The Sorrows of Young Werther* is secretly autobiography," I tell him.

"But that was actually a fiction!" he protests. "Certainly the structure contains autobiographical elements, but I made everything else up!"

"Well," I say. "Maybe it was easier reading. I mean, after all, your autobiography is, what? Thirteen volumes?"

He answers: "That's what I needed to get to the truth."

I suggest: "Possibly Young Werther is what you needed to get to the poetry."

"Ach," he shakes his head. "Perhaps we shall never resolve this."

"Well then," I say, stretching after a long sit down. "Möchten Sie ein paar Bier trinken? Would you like to drink a few beers?"

"Ja. Natürlich. A brilliant idea! Wir zu den Biergarten gehen."

Arm in arm we stroll to the beer garden, and as we stroll we sing: *Du, du liegst mir im Herzen,* the song about the man whose heart breaks because his great love cannot take him seriously.

James Boswell's *Life of Samuel Johnson,* LL.D. published in 1791

They meet at a bookstore, but it doesn't go well.

Boswell: "I apologize for being a Scot. I cannot help it."

Johnson: "That, Sir, I find, is what a very great many of your country-men cannot help."

See "Bozzy" of a morning enjoying a public hanging, darting down an alley for quick sex, and later, a fervid night in public or private house playing the buffoon, worse for drink. How could this besotted poltroon produce such a work of light and intelligence?

Well, Macaulay says in 1831, that dolt didn't exactly write the Life, he merely took it down: faithful, mindless stenographer. The Biography has merits, he concludes, but only a fool could have written it.

Later, however, the attics and closets of Boswell descendants in Scotland and Ireland open. Manuscript caches take flight, caught up by the universities. Boswell is recognized an exigent writer, not at all vapid, prepared by life for the great work, the superb Biography.

Johnson, moral and intellectual touchstone, now slumps in a grubby corner, mistranslated into something else: Hapless literary marionette.

"Do us a little dance, will ye?" leers lubricious Bozzy.

Johnson arises, clears his throat—ever ready with a snappy quotation.

House on West 35th Street

A woman I'd met had read the thirty-three novels and thirty-nine short stories about Nero Wolfe, the detective, more than once—in fact, again and again—as I had. More than the stories themselves, we agreed, it was their backdrop that drew us to them: the old brownstone on West 35th Street, the seven stone steps to the front door. The one-way glass allowing those ringing to be identified by those inside. Then, inside, the massive walnut coat rack, the rarely used front room. On the right, the dining room (lunch 1:15 pm; dinner 7:15 pm); the elevator, used by Wolfe to reach his orchids—10,000 of them!—on the top floor. (His orchid tending schedule: from 9:00 am to 11:00; 4:00 pm to 6:00). Further down, near the kitchen, the office with its leather-bound books, its wooden globe three feet in diameter. Then the kitchen, where Fritz prepares exquisite meals. Inside the refrigerator and larder, one knew one would find the most exquisite stuff. It is not the stories that we care about, but the house itself: its clocklike regularity that invites us out of our clinking, clock-screwy lives.

But I'm unsettled to discover a rival to that old place. Now when I'd enter the house and she'd be there; or I'd be alone, and she might appear and startle me. I begin to assess her—this trespasser of sacred space between eyes and printed page. And, looking at her, I see suspicion, too: her shifting eyes, her lips curling, about to snarl in Wolfe's lair.

Tomas Tranströmer and Robert Bly
Translate Each Other's Poems

Tranströmer writes: "You changed my line to: 'The plow lifts from the furrow like an owl slowly airborne,' but what I meant was: 'The plow lifts the furrow like an owl crushing rocks.' Well, I like yours better in English, so please use it that way." Bly writes, "My English word 'headlong' means 'rushing at something heedlessly.' But I like it that you've translated it as 'He grows a head of enormous length.' I send you several new pages of verse that go in the direction you've pointed out."

Meanwhile, where there are no negotiations:

Khrushchev thunders in 1956: "We will bury you!" after the Soviets explode an H-Bomb, and the Cold War is ratcheted up. But the correct translation should have been, "We will outlast you."

In 1945 Truman demands that the Japanese surrender. Japan issues a statement that it will consider the demand, but it's mistranslated: "We're ignoring you with contempt." Ten days later, thousands die at Hiroshima.

Early in the first millennium, Saint Jerome translates the story of Moses returning from the mountain with horns on his head, having been hung with them by the Lord. But "horns" could be translated as "a great light on his face." Yet, for more than one thousand years, Jews are believed to descend from Satan. Millions are killed.

Can poetry matter?

A Lecture from the Bartender at Grand Hotel, Oslo

Translation is difficult. We don't expect our American tourists to speak Norwegian so we learn English. One language can do violence to the other. Pick its pocket, so to speak.

For instance, Oslo gets many meters of snowfall. Knut Hamsun, in *Hunger*, has his character sleeping in the snowed-in streets of Kristiania. (Oslo was called Kristiania in 1899.) Hamsun knew those streets. But then your Robert Bly comes along with his egregious English translation and messes up the map so that it neither resembles Kristiania nor Oslo. A tourist could get lost in the snow and die following Mr. Bly's map! Knut Hamsun was our breakthrough novelist and maybe deserves more respect, though he was often down and out.

Henrik Ibsen was our breakthrough dramatist—hardly down and out!—but you wouldn't know it from the English translations.

For instance, in *Ghosts*, Mrs. Alving refers to her husband lying around reading "bank journals," which doesn't make any sense in English. But Norwegians know instantly that "bank journals" really means "pornography."

Ibsen drank and dined at the Cafe every night. His dinner was always an open sandwich, beer and schnapps. And often a *pjolter*, which is our word for Whisky and Soda.

And he could get very drunk!

Hamsun and Ibsen lived here in Kristiania at the same time, and I think they met only once, poverty and wealth being discrete languages.

One night Ibsen was too drunk to sit. He insulted the waiters and we had to translate him into the street.

Hamsun was down and out, living in a wooden crate outside the Cafe. Ibsen landed next to him and decided to take a little nap. Then you could see Hamsun's arm reach out of the box and pick Ibsen's pocket!

Then Hamsun translated himself into the Cafe and ordered a splendid supper!

MAX'S—How History Is Made

—for Amy Wallace

"I hated travelling," Max, author of best-selling travel guides and an occasional host of a BBC radio program about travel, said. "After a lifetime of trekking from airport to castle to pretentious B & B, I realized I disliked people, foreign cities, even the food. So I came up with a scheme—a *technique*—which allowed me to do my travel writing from home."

We were seated on the patio of a hotel at Cortina d'Ampezzo in the Italian Dolomites where Max lived. The sun, reflected from the ski slopes, was shining directly on him, the light glaring so that I could barely make out his features. But I had begged him to tell me how he had become a successful travel writer and he had agreed he would.

I started in a small way *(he said)*. I was a compiler of tourist information for a travel agency back in New Jersey, which specialized in putting tours together for the elderly. I was bored with the job, listing all the sights of Rome, the names of the great emperors, details so tedious I was sure no one would pay any attention. But my employer insisted I produce yards and yards of that stuff. So for my personal amusement, I added the names of my friends to the list of Ancient Poets, which included Dante and Homer. The brochure was published and I waited for the second shoe to drop, so to speak, but no one caught on to what I'd done.

That made me bolder. Why not go beyond imaginative lists in my guides? For fun, why not fabricate art objects supposedly to be found in recondite Roman alleys or spurious churches? Without giving the exact address, I invented an ancient statue of Adam, naked, dancing and waving over his head a ten-gallon cowboy hat. Next, in a description of the Fountain of Trevi, into which tourists make wishes, throw coins, and even swim when drunk, I claimed that the beautiful fountain once had been a secret waste treatment facility. ("Let the tourists muck about in that for awhile," I thought.)

Still, no one called me on the carpet for what I'd written. In fact, my boss heard back from customers who praised the exciting details, apparently not to be found elsewhere. "You should write a guidebook," he told me. "I think you've got something, a writing talent that drums up business. You write one and I'll publish it."

We worked out an arrangement. He would pay me to travel around— to destinations that his agency wanted to sell—and I could write what I liked as long as I got the tourists there. For instance, I took on the hotels of New York's Borscht belt, deserted during the winters, where famous comedians had once played. With a little research and imagination I put together a program that included the last living comics (hired for pennies), as well as promises of appearances by the ghosts of more famous ones. (Screenings of the famous comics' films.) This turned out to be a financial success, so he sent me on to Europe.

Here I encountered my first problem: foreign languages. My bosses' elderly tourists would be uncomfortable if they couldn't communicate in English. I toyed with the silly idea of finding a small, unknown country, such as an Andorra, a Liechtenstein, or a San Marino, and declaring that their second language was something everyone knew, like Pig Latin. But this, I realized, was silly and unnecessary. Everyone I met in Europe at the hotels and restaurants spoke English.

In any case, I wrote on, borrowing heavily from published tourist guides and inventing my whimsical, impossible to find highlights. There was a certain kind of tourist, I learned, who was content with the standard foreign city tours if his reading up on those cities was salted with a bit of fancy, things he could imagine without the extra footsteps and stair climbs it would take to actually see them. I made doubly sure that all my little marvels were located just out of reach. I soon found that my formula of travel and fantasy allowed me to put together a winning tourist product.

It finally got to the point when I didn't need to travel at all. By studying published travel guides I'd cull their obscure facts, locate some unknown town off the railway line, some area too remote to reach, and let my imagination go to work.

Naturally, you might think that my inventions were nothing more than private jokes that added spice to the tourist routine. But one incident, recently, proved to me that, by giving free rein to my imagination, I was unleashing forces more powerful than I'd ever imagined.

Once in a while I was obligated to take VIPs on authoritative visits to foreign locales personally. On this trip I found myself escorting a bunch of VIPs around the mountain resorts of the Trentino-Alto Adige in Northern Italy.

On my tour group's last day with me, I accompanied them to the railroad station in Trento. While they boarded trains to Venice and Verona, I waved goodbye and decided to treat myself to a long lunch in the tratoria near the Giordano.

The owner and his wife were extremely friendly, and I enjoyed the food and wine. Late in the afternoon, when I thought I'd better pay my bill and tell them goodbye before I fell over my chair, I asked the owner when he thought the next train would be along.

He told me that the Balzano train would arrive soon. I asked if the station sold guide books to the area. He gave me a quizzical smile and wondered why I, the travel expert would need one when I had documented the area so famously. "For back-up," I told him cryptically.

Imagine my surprise when I found that the station news kiosk sold only one travel guide: my own. But I bought a copy. Why not see where this takes me? I asked myself, no doubt my reason affected by the wine.

I boarded the train to Balzano, and then leisurely inspected the map of stations along the way. Only one of them sparked memory: Merano, the tenth stop on the journey (not counting the Trento Goods Station).

What had caught my eye about Merano? According to me (well, at least according to the guides I'd cribbed) snow covered the mountains and palm trees were to be found in the valleys. A world chess championship had been held there. And so on. Merano was a city, too accessible a locale for my imaginative efforts, which required remoteness and inaccessbility.

But tracing the map I stopped at another name that rang a louder bell: the village of Vilpiano. What had I written about it? "Vilpiano is a district of Terlan, which is well-known especially for asparagus." To most travelers that description might not be compelling. But I recognized it as ideal: a few buildings and farms, and a place where the imaginative travel-artist might paint in a happy little tree or a swirling flock of seraph'ed doves to enhance the picture.

In fact, I did remember what I'd invented for that town; one of my better efforts, I congratulated myself: an imposing and exotic gaming hall in the middle of nowhere. I decided to make a visit and see what was actually to be seen there.

Conceive of my surprise, then, when the train pulled into the rustic station at Vilpiano, and I saw parking lots full of cars and people milling around the piazza, most heading toward a large, fascist-era building lit with neon signs. Was today a saint's *festa*? I asked myself. (Hadn't I included a schedule of them in one of my books?) Was it a national holiday? (Ditto, I had a chart somewhere that might tell me.) Surely, today must be some holiday, and that building must be a *birreria*: a beer hall. I couldn't remember. So, along with everyone, I let myself be drawn into the piazza toward the old building.

As soon as I was pushed through the doorway I froze in place, resisting the people milling around me. From the look of it, this was not some country *birreria*, but a sophisticated entertainment palace, with gambling tables, slot machines, and hanging from the ceiling, multiple trapezes on which naked young women were swinging leisurely. The most astounding thing to me was that, not only did this place resemble the extravaganza I'd invented for my travel guide; every detail of furnishing, color, even the lighting, was exactly as I'd imagined it.

You will understand if I tell you that I was overcome. How was this possible? Had I read about the place before writing my book, forgotten that I'd read, then "invented" it? Or had something else happened? Could I even consider it seriously? That my word had become flesh? Had I, for an obscure Italian town, willed into existence this glitzy, gaudy, glorious palace—this bordello of someone's dream?

Across the floor I saw an elegant bar. I found a chair and ordered a grappa. I got the same look of recognition from the barman that I'd become familiar with since my face appeared on the cover of my guides. He poured and handed me the glass. "This is with our compliments," he told me. "But excuse me for just a moment." And he walked away.

I sat and sipped my grappa. Imagine yourself in my situation. What would you make of this? Wasn't it more likely that I had read about this place and forgotten it? More likely, I mean, than entertaining the thought that by my imaginative power I had somehow created this thing out of ... nothing? But if I did have those powers, shouldn't I consider, just for a moment, what else I might invent? If my power were the genie in the lamp, what should I conjure for myself, or—let me be generous— for the world?

My daydream was interrupted when the barman returned with another. This fellow, dressed in a gaudy and theatrical smoking jacket, looked like an actor playing the part of the "proprietor." And, when the barman introduced him to me, that is exactly who he turned out to be—not an actor, the actual proprietor.

"Mr. Max," he said with an immense smile. "It is my great pleasure to welcome you! We've all been hoping for this moment. So tell me," the owner said, gesturing with his hands the vastness of the room. "Do you approve?"

I admit I was frozen. All I could muster was a stammering, "What is this place?"

Now the proprietor seemed confused. "But," he told me, "it is your place. MAX's!" And he lifted his arms and his hands pointed above our heads to a huge sign of pulsing, blaring light that I could barely keep in focus: "*MAX'S.*"

I looked at the sign, at my name in fifty foot high lights, and was silenced. Happily, though, the proprietor recognized my confusion and hastened to explain: "You see," he said. "We built it to your specifications—to your description of it in your guidebook."

"Why?" I asked, still rigid.

"Well, you see," the proprietor explained, "Vilpiano has no modern industry. Once, there was bauxite mining, but when that was exhausted, we thought we were finished. Things were going downhill financially.

But then one day I was travelling to Milano. In a kiosk I saw your book about Northern Italy. Imagine my surprise when I read your description of our town! What an idea to attract tourists! I returned home and found investors who loved your vision, as I did. It took some time, but we finished converting this old railroad building into a modern entertainment palace. And, as you see, the tourists have come. Right now, they are locals, but with success we imagine we'll attract the international crowd. And of course," he finished, "we would be most grateful if, in a future edition of your esteemed guide, you'd write some more about our marvelous tourist attraction right here—this place named in your honor: MAX'S."

Later when I was able to reflect, it all made sense. This was not the *Twilight Zone* after all. I was not so much disappointed by Vilpiano, but damn angry! Angry because they had stolen my ideas!

After I found my voice again, I protested loudly. The proprietor, to console me, insisted I stay and enjoy the pleasures of the place.

I stayed and ate and drank and indulged myself to the point where, after a week or so, I had made myself sick. That was inevitable, of course. Anyone gorging so immoderately on his own imagination would get ill. But I did have a long moment of revelation: Where was I? Enjoying a place conjured in my fantasy but made into something real by a stranger; a simulacrum of myself, but lost to me. And who was I? In a life of indulgent fantasy and happy accident I had nearly obliterated myself. I OWN MY OWN! I had shouted at the Dolomites in my distress, but there was never a resounding, reassuring echo.

"In any case," Max said, "'I am back, enjoying this hotel in my retirement. And you? Did you say you planned to follow me, to write travel guides?"

"I would like to do that, yes."

The sun, ricocheting off the snow banks, continued to obscure my view of him, as if he were struggling to remain visible.

"Well, don't steal any of my ideas like those bastards in Vilpiano. They're all copyrighted."

Foreign Tongue

I. The Belluno Language School

"I urge you not to bother," Max said when I told him I wanted to learn Italian. "Some people—and I'm looking right at you—can't be taught. But, if you insist, I'll recommend a language school."

At his direction, I rented a car, an old limousine, the only vehicle available during that high season. Max took his place in the back, an obscure, saturnine figure hidden in shadows. I took the chauffer's wheel, and we were off to Belluno, at the base of the mountain, and the Belluno Language School.

Craig, the school's director, explained how it worked. "Ya see," he said with a Cockney accent, "we teach one-on-one, or, at the most, two students at a time. We never use the student's native language. From the first class our instructors speak nothing but Italian. Let me show you how this works."

He invited me to put on headphones and look through a panel into the classroom, where two well-dressed, obviously American women were taking their first lesson. "These ladies came over to shop in the fashionable stores of Milan and Rome. Even though most everyone in business in Italy speaks English, these ladies think they'll get the best bargains if they know the native tongue."

I listened as the instructor began the lesson. "Questa è un tavalo," he said, pointing to a table. "Repeta."

Silence from the students.

"Repeta: Questa è un tavalo."

One woman turned to the other: "What's he want us to do?"

The other: "I have no idea."

The instructor repeated the phrase. It was obvious that he wanted the women to repeat it.

One woman held up her hands: "I don't know what he's saying. Can't he speak English?"

The other: "Beats me."

With his index finger, Max touched the skin under his eye, pulling it down, as if opening it wider, an Italian gesture. "As I said, foreign languages are impossible for some people."

II. Saving the World

Craig specialized in teaching English to Italians.

"The English laugh at us Cheapsiders, us Cockneys," he said. "But I've come up with a new way to teach my students English. My way, they learn three times as many words then the usual teaching method. Here, I'll show you."

He introduced me to Gian, one of his students. "Tell us," he said to Gian in Italian, "tell us about that man you see walking down that street."

Gian eyed the man for awhile, chuckled, and then spoke in English: "'E's wearin' a syrup! Nearly knocked me off me plates, it did!"

Craig smiled contentedly. "Did you get it? No? Well, it's really very simple. You could tell of course that that man in the street was wearing a wig? A big floppy thing. So Gian correctly pointed out that the man was wearing a syrup, which is Cockney rhyming slang for wig: 'syrup of figs', or just 'syrup'."

"What about the 'plates'?"

"What he was saying was that seeing the man in the wig nearly knocked him off his feet. In Cockney, 'feet' is 'plates of meat.'"

"Yar," Gian said. "I couldn't believe me mincers!"

I looked at Craig.

"Eyes," said Craig. "'Couldn't believe my eyes. 'Minced pies' equal 'eyes'." You see, for every English word they learn, they've got to learn at least two others to speak the slang. It's a very efficient method."

Gian was smiling at me, happy to have had the opportunity to demonstrate.

Craig confided: "I predict Gian will learn so well he'll pass the government exam."

"What does he want to do?"

"To be one of those translators at the UN. You know, help with the nuclear disarmament."

III. Italian Gibberish

"You sound like Robert," Max said after I'd demonstrated my newly learned Italian to him. "He worked at the hotel last year. He *thought* he could speak the language but no one could understand him. He mouthed a lot of syllables that sounded like Italian words, but they were just gibberish. One day I foolishly let him speak to an Italian tourist group I was guiding. They thought he was an utter moron."

After a frustrating session, the group settled in for lunch at a restaurant in the hotel. No one wanted to sit next to him. But after they'd eaten, Robert, still confused—he really believed he could speak Italian—wandered off and found a piano in the hallway. He began to play a lonely bit of Mozart. Since he was actually an excellent pianist, everyone stopped talking to listen. When he'd finished, the Italians, who had gathered around, gave him enthusiastic applause. Robert was startled by the unexpected appreciation, but happy.

IV. Falling In Love

One of my Italian friends invited me to dinner at his parents' home. There, he introduced me to his cousin Costanzia, a beautiful girl with bright dark eyes, silken skin, and a small waist. I fell in love.

"Do you want to worship at her feet?" my friend asked me, snickering. "Watch out! We call her the Blessed Virgin."

"Yes," I confessed. "I want to die in her arms."

"You should be very careful. She's not sophisticated. Very prudish, like all Italian girls. You could try talking to her, though. She speaks no English. You'll have to use your Italian. It will be good for you both. Try."

I said in Italian: "I'm very sorry that my Italian is no good, but I only took lessons for a few weeks."

She asked where I'd studied. I told her. She asked where I lived and what was it like? That was more difficult since my Italian consisted of only about one hundred words, and I had to stitch them together the best I could, as well as bring in the Latin I'd learned in high school. It was vigorous mental exercise, and ultimately frustrating.

Even so, she shouted happily to a friend in another room, "I can understand him!"

But I was running out of Italian words. "You don't speak any English?" I asked, hoping she had at least a few.

She shook her head sadly.

Then I had an idea. It was an opportunity. I'd say in English what I truly felt about her without having to worry about negative consequences. "You are the most beautiful woman I've ever seen." I told her. "I would love to put my arms around you and kiss you with all my soul and take you down on this floor and have mad sex with you right now!"

She looked at me, her eyes on mine, stepped closer and kissed me on the lips—a deep, soulful, erotic kiss. Then, with an enigmatic smile, she turned and left the room.

The Tour Guide Describes Van Gogh In Arles:
How History Is Made

"This is the courtyard of the Hospital at Arles. The painter Van Gogh was hospitalized here after slicing his ear, a bizarre gift for a prostitute. He made about 150 pictures while in this hospital, including the famous view of the courtyard, featuring the garden and central fish pond. Of course, after Van Gogh made this picture in April 1889, the hospital was often renovated. But many years ago, when Van Gogh's reputation had grown—and consequently was bringing crowds of tourists to Arles—the city recognized the value of maintaining the buildings and landscape as represented in Van Gogh's painting. After years of meticulous reconstruction, the painting and the garden are again identical. Thus, we have two views of history: When Van Gogh painted his painting he was representing history, no matter what else he was doing. Now, in the interests of tourism, we have history representing his painting."

(How History Is Not Made:
Sherlock Holmes Predicts the Outcome of W.W. I

The two friends chatted in intimate converse for a few minutes, recalling once again the days of the past, while their prisoner vainly wriggled to undo the bonds that held him. As they turned to the car Holmes pointed back to the moonlit sea and shook a thoughtful head. "There's an east wind coming, Watson."

"I think not, Holmes. It is very warm."

"Good old Watson! You are the one fixed point in a changing age. There's an east wind coming all the same, such a wind as never blew on England yet. It will be cold and bitter, Watson and a good many of us may wither before its blast. But it's God's own wind none the less, and a cleaner, better, stronger land will lie in the sunshine when the storm has cleared. Start her up, Watson, for it's time that we were on our way." —Arthur Conan Doyle, "His Last Bow" 1917.)

Argol Karvarkian, *Otiose Warts.*
(Bergen: Univ. of University Press. 2015)

This forty-fifth collection continues Karvarkian's obsession with minia-
ture poetics: lyrics gorgeously wrought, each with the grace and identi-
calness of a Faberge egg. It is curious that after Karvarkian's decades of
writing and publishing well-mannered volumes, his many readers may
not recall his earliest work, which is characterized by a surprisingly prim-
itive, even brutish sensibility. A far cry from the lapidary incrustations
of his contemporary work, his earlier poems seem to have originated in
a swamp: metaphors dense as quagmire, often expressed in grunts, such
as "Bleep. Fsssssh. Poof." Contrast this with the minimalist clarity and
grace of a lyrical refrain from a poem in his newest collection: "This.
That. This."

I first met Karvarkian in Florida. I had recently married, and my wife
and I shared a shack on stilts in an obscure part of the Everglades, where
I could work on my literary criticism in solitude. Karvarkian was young,
of course, with massive, unkempt hair and musky odor. The three of us
became friends after we'd met at the local fishing-themed gastropub in
town. Gradually, I began to notice the attraction Karvarkian and my
wife shared, and so I wasn't surprised when one day he took me aside
and growled, "I'm leaving on a lengthy journey to reach the end of the
world. And, oh yes, do you mind if I take your wife?" He was surprised, I
surmise, by my gracious accession.

In those days there seemed to be an endless supply of wives in the
Everglades, so I had no trouble marrying again. What did astound me,
however, was that within a month of my second marriage Karvarkian
reappeared, his long trip apparently cut short. He pointed his finger at
my trembling first wife. "I don't like this one," he told me. "But your
new one seems entirely lovable. Do you mind if I take her along on my
infinite journey?" Naturally, I greatly protested. Wasn't one enough for
him? But my new wife flashed her eyes and I obliged her.

This left me in rather an awkward position. My first wife and I were no longer properly married, but she didn't seem to be leaving the house, so we resumed our cohabitation with the proviso that I might at any time, should I wish, take a new wife. Eventually I did.

It was then that Karvarkian once again reentered our lives. "Take this one back," he ordered, thrusting my second wife at me. "Lemme have the new one." Numbed, I could only allow her to go.

Now I was living with two former wives. After some time, I remarried. Moments after that ceremony, as if he'd been lurking beneath a trap door, Karvarkian abruptly appeared demanding the new wife in trade for the old.

This pattern continued for some years. Eventually I stopped protesting because I'd begun to notice that after each exchange of wives a new book of Karvarkian's poetry would appear. Each time, I would read it with immense interest and greatly marvel at his progression of intellect and technique from volume to volume.

His eighteenth collection, *Phlogiston, You Betcha*, evidences what we might call the typical Karvarkian poem of the early middle period: odd language and budding obsession with the mysterious *shadow figure*, eventually to be known as the *Procurer*, so famously developed in later volumes:

> A can of f*****g beer
> *collides with a f*****g cold thought:*
> *Pimp me vittles,*
> *that little b******d*
> *better deliver*
> *me f*****g flame-retardant*
> *flapdoodle another beer*
> *in f*****g skirts*
> *or I crush his f*****g*
> *smooch.* ("A Bone Aren't Made of Beer")

By his thirtieth volume, *We'll Burn That Bridge Before We Even Think of It*, his outlandish verbosity has given way to a diction both natural and unforced:

> The notion of amber gosling waddling,
> my sainted Procurer
> in his red wheelbarrow.
> "Ducky," I coo. "Get me another
> in her flowing skirts. This one's gone dry."
> Gosling nestles, but tiresome Procurer
> demands recompense.
> Grudgingly,
> I flip him the bird. ("The Pushover Prize")

Although I presently support forty-six ex-wives on the meager receipts of my modest critical efforts, I can't help but believe that I had something to do with the great Karvarkian's evolution as a poet. After all, he seemed to extract a tangible grace from the women I married—and, I flatter myself—possibly because of my own connection to them. I'd also like to think that my judicially crafted critical prose—which my wives have assured me they read aloud to him each evening—have helped to discipline his earlier poetic unruliness.

I can think of no better evidence of this than this latest volume. Here he demonstrates, with a directness characteristic of his formative earlier work, what may be a final, summative reconciling with the Procurer, the mysterious shadow-figure:

> Needles, needles.
> Glockenspiel headstrong.
> Ale may ail and skirt hurt,
> but o my sissy-brother,
> there is nary the consumer
> absent the consumed. ("Elapsed Bumbershoot")

Whether this mysterious *Procurer* will ever be brought fully from the shadows must wait on future Karvarkian collections, although significant criticism has already appeared. (See my *The Mysterious Procurer in the Poetry of Karvarkian*. Three volumes. Freemont: Univ. of University Press. 2010)

Still, if we are to consider the totality of Argol Karvarkian's oeuvre, we must ask, what does it signify? What will be its influence? These beautiful Faberge egg-like poems, several dozen to a package: how are we to understand such exigent fragility? I think, in the end, they will share the fate of all delicately created things. Like Faberge eggs they will abide as objects that we can admire, but that, once having admired, we relegate to our collector's shelf without further comment.

Acknowledgements

Grateful acknowledgement is made to the following where these works originally appeared, mostly in different versions:

"A Hamptons Apprenticeship: Pictures From A Place and Year," adopted and expanded from "Hamptons Found and Lost: A Memoir with Reviews." *Confrontation* No.70/71. Winter/Spring 2000.

"Meeting H. R. Hays," excerpted from "H.R. Hays: The Theater of Disappointment," *Talisman: A Journal of Contemporary Poetry and Poetics,* Issue #43, 2015. (A partial history of H. R. Hays' work in the theater with Bertolt Brecht, Kurt Weill, and others.)

"Remembering H.R. Hays." *Poetry Bay* September 2000

"David Ignatow: Notes On a Small Song," excerpted from: "With Ignatow," *Sentence: A Journal of Prose Poetics No. 2, Firewheel Editions, 2004;* "David Ignatow: Notes On A Small Song." *Descant* 102, Vol. 29, No. 3. Fall 1998; "Fond Memories of a Poet-Mentor." *The New York Times.* November 30, 1997

"Charles Matz : Chaos," Charles Matz taped interview, Jan 21, 2012; "Introduction," *Performance*, Charles Matz, New York: Survivors Manual Books, 1978

"John Hall Wheelock: A Brief Return," *Marsh Hawk Review* November 2015. "Ilya Bolotowsky: The Bubble Reputation" excerpted from: "Taking Reality Through Its Paces: Filmmaking With Norman Mailer and Ilya Bolotowsky." *Confrontation* No. 80/81, Fall 2002/Winter 2003 (A full treatment of the film Bolotowsky/Mailer film.)

"Robert Bly's Light and Sound" including excerpts from "Robert Bly vs. the First Ten Issues of *kayak,*" *Galatea Resurrects*, November 2014

"Tomas Tranströmer and Robert Bly Translate Each Other's Poems," "Hemingway Completes His Introduction to *A Moveable Feast*," "The Plagiarist's Heart." *Otoliths*, November 2015

"A Lecture from the Bartender at Grand Hotel, Oslo," *Red Ochre Lit*, 2012. Japanese version Tokyo: *Quince Wharf,* Natsuko Hirata, trans., 2012 "James Boswell's Life of Samuel Johnson, LL.D. published in 1791," "Goethe Writes *Aus meinem Leben: Dichtung und Wahrheit* (1811–1833)," *Marsh Hawk Review*, 2012

"Tunneling Into the Next Life: Three Hamptons Poets and Their Final Work," (works cited: David Ignatow. *Living Is What I Wanted: Last Poems*. Rochester: Boa Editions. 1999; Armand Schwerner. *Selected Shorter Poems*. San Diego: Junction Press. 1999; *The Tablets*; Orono: The National Poetry Foundation. 1999; Harvey Shapiro. *A Momentary Glory: Last Poems*. Middletown: Wesleyan. 2014)

NOTES

A desire to understand issues concerning the lives of my mentors has resulted in several literary projects: a history of the stage work, translation and poetry of H. R. Hays, the compilation and transcription of print and television interviews with Hays, David Ignatow and Charles Matz, and the present book.

Contributors *to* The Bonacker

Eliot Atkinson, ceramics; Robert A. Aurthur, television and short story writer; Charles Boltenhouse, dance writer; John Cole Jr., fiction; Oscar Collier, painter and writer; Avril Dayton, college student—first publication; Henry Gilfond, radio writer; H. R. Hays; William Iverson, radio producer; Barbara Leslie Jordan, poet; Eunice Jackett, journalist and travel writer; Joseph Liss, television and radio writer; Frank O'Hara, poet; Ann Porter, writer and painter; Fairfield Porter, painter; Jeffrey Potter, theater; Dorothy Quick, syndicated newspaper columnist; Lynn Riggs, Broadways musicals; Larry Rivers, painter; May D. Rogers, poet and journalist; Mary Soles, first poetry publication; William Soles, ceramics; May Natalie Tabak, contributor to *Commentary*; Parker Tyler, poet and journalist; John Hall Wheelock, poet and editor; and Kazamiers Wierzynski, published 23 books in Polish and several in English.

Informal list of notables buried in Green River Cemetery, Springs, East Hampton

James Brooks (painter) (1906–1992)—abstract painter; Dan Christensen (1942–2007)—artist; Fred Coe (1914–1979)—television producer of The Philco Television Playhouse; Stuart Davis (1892[94?]–1964)—cubist artist; Elaine de Kooning (1918–1989)—artist and wife of abstract expressionist Willem de Kooning, who is not buried there; Jimmy Ernst (1920–1984)—artist and son of Max Ernst; Pierre Franey (1921–1996)—chef and newspaper columnist; John Ferren (1905–1970)—painter; Henry Geldzahler (1935–1994)—art historian, critic, museum curator and NYC Commissioner of Cultural Affairs; Charles Gwathmey (1938–2009)—architect;

Lee Krasner (1908–1984)—artist and wife of Jackson Pollock; Ibram Lassaw (1913–2003)—abstract sculptor; William S. Lieberman (1923–2005)—Museum of Modern Art curator; A.J. Liebling (1904–1963)—newspaper columnist; Jan Yoors (1922–1977)—artist and writer; Hilda Morley (1916–1998)—poet; Frank O'Hara (1926–1966)—poet; Alfonso A. Ossorio (1916–1990)—artist (half his ashes are here); Alan Pakula (1928–1998)—film producer of *To Kill a Mockingbird*, film director of *Klute* and *All the President's Men*; Jackson Pollock (1912–1956)—abstract expressionist painter and husband of Lee Krasner; Abraham Rattner (1895–1978)—painter; Ad Reinhardt (1913–1967)—abstract painter; Harold Rosenberg (1906–1978)—art critic; Steven J. Ross (1927–1992)—CEO who engineered the merger of Time-Warner; Jean Stafford (1915–1979)—Pulitzer Prize–winning writer; Stan Vanderbeek (1927–1983)—underground film maker; Hannah Wilke (1940–1993)—painter, sculptor and photographer; Stefan Wolpe (1902–1972)—composer; Gary McFarland (1933–1971)—musician, composer, producer; Peter Boyle (1935–2006)—actor.

About the Author

THE AUTHOR WITH H. R. HAYS, 1970

SANDY MCINTOSH was born in Rockville Centre, New York, and received a BA from Southampton College, an MFA from Columbia University and a PhD. from the Union Graduate School. After working with children for eight years as a writer in the schools of Long Island's East End, Nassau County and in Brooklyn, he completed a study of writers who taught in the program and how their work with children affected their own writing. The study, *The Poets in the Poets-in-the Schools* was published by the University of Minnesota. For fifteen years he taught creative writing at Long Island University and Hofstra University while publishing nonfiction works, such as *Firing Back* (John Wiley & Sons), and computer software, such as *Mavis Beacon Teaches Typing!* (Electronic Arts,). He has contributed journalism, poetry, and opinion columns to *The New York Times*, *Newsday*, *The Nation*, *The Wall Street Journal*, *The Long Island Press*, *American Book Review*, and elsewhere. He was also editor and publisher of *Wok Talk*, a Chinese cooking bi-monthly and the author and editor of several Chinese cook books and one of the first cooking software computer programs.

His first collection of poetry, *Earth Works*, was published by Southampton College in 1970, the year he graduated. He has since published six poetry collections: *Which Way to the Egress?* (1974), *Endless Staircase* (1994), *Between Earth and Sky* (2002), *The After-Death History of My Mother* (2005), *Forty-Nine Guaranteed Ways to Escape Death* (2007), *Ernesta, in the Style of the Flamenco* (2010) and also a collaboration with the poet Denise Duhamel, *237 More Reasons to Have Sex* (2009). His recent collection, *Cemetery Chess: Selected and New Poems*, was published in 2012.

His original poetry in a screenplay won the Silver Medal in the Film Festival of the Americas. Recently, *The New York Times'* web edition published his poem "Cemetery Chess," and an excerpt of his collaboration with Denise Duhamel appears in *The Best American Poetry*.

He was Managing Editor of Long Island University's national literary journal, *Confrontation*. For more than a decade he was a host of Riverhead Cablevision's TV series, "Ideas and Issues." He is currently publisher of Marsh Hawk Press.

About the Cover Artist

KEN ROBBINS is a fine art photographer, commercial artist, and the writer/illustrator of more than twenty highly acclaimed children's books, has been living and making photographs in East Hampton, New York since 1972. He was born in Brooklyn, New York, in 1945, raised in West Orange, New Jersey, and graduated Cornell University in 1967 with a degree in English. After five years as a book editor in New York City, he moved to the East End of Long Island, and commenced a freelance career that continues today. He lives in Springs with his wife, Maria.

About the Author's Other Books

Between Earth and Sky

What a treat. I had to stop myself from reading *Between Earth and Sky* straight through like a novel so I'd have something saved to look forward to. I don't like people calling writing 'gorgeous' but it really is gorgeous writing. One of the very best things about this collection, for me, is that it's approachable. So much of it is just wonderfully lyrical and funny and moving. What a crazy/delicious world McIntosh invents.—LANFORD WILSON, **winner of the Pulitzer Prize**

"With a surrealist's touch, Sandy McIntosh wickedly maps out the psyche's contradictions and movingly explores family pain and grief. His clean, swift poems strike the reader's eye as well as heart as they rangle from hope to nightmare, from loss to social comedy".—MICHAEL HELLER

Endless Staircare

With *Endless Staircase*, Sandy McIntosh distinguishes himself as a significant new talent. His sardonic, often wild humor is the path into very serious personal, social and quite frequently religious/philosophical concerns. I have been genuinely surprised by a voice I have never before heard in matters of such weight and intensity.—DAVID IGNATOW, **winner of the Bollingen Prize**

Forty-Nine Guaranteed Ways to Escape Death

"Wow! It is an *estro dis-armonico*. The energy is straight from the astral black holes. Iconoclastic right in-your-face. Velvet gloves of colloquial and elite language covering a skillful dissecting hand. An arsenal of erudite weapons used pitilessly... or so it seems".—CHARLES MATZ, **Chevalier de la Legion d'Honneur, France.**

Cemetery Chess: Selected and New Poems

Sandy McIntosh's *Cemetery Chess: Selected and New Poems* is intelligent, funny, well-crafted, and just fun to read. McIntosh's work has been around in the background for me for quite a while. I knew of it, but I did not know it well; thus, this book comes as a welcome introduction to the scope of his poetic arc. His work is strikingly clear, but with a clarity that comes from a place that throws us off kilter, for it seems that he is looking at daily life with more insightful eyes than ours. The poems are filled with places and people, especially artist and poets--Eileen Tabios gets her own poem! McIntosh's poems are serious pieces that are not pretentious, just pieces from a sharp mind. —WILLIAM ALLEGREZZA, *Goodreads*

The After-Death History of My Mother

Sandy McIntosh's entertaining new volume might be mistaken, at first, for a merry romp through personal and literary history conducted by a slightly confused, well-meaning people-pleaser. His confusion begins with his bemused revelation that he has (maybe) two mothers, and continues through various other doublings (dream transformations, reincarnations, literary 'forgeries,' literary mothers both male and female, poems masquerading as prose and vice versa) to a final doubling (double-crossing) that brings with it a 'broade [sic] awaking' to reality.... This is a book of elegies—eulogies, really—to all the literal and literary bastards who have made McIntosh an artist and (maybe) a con. —LAURAL BLOSSOM, *American Book Review*

The showcase piece of this book, a long sequence titled "Obsessional," is remarkable for yoking an engaging Elizabethan literary detective story to a personal narrative about life as a grad school poet. Even more impressive than this set-up actually succeeding is the way McIntosh is able to tie compassion to dagger-thrust humor. If that's what "obsessional" poetry is—personal narrative of neurosis that is aware a world exists outside the poet's gut, and is not afraid to tell a joke—maybe it will catch on among those still in the stranglehold of the confessional. The ending sequence is balanced at the front of the book by the title sequence, composed of memorial lyrics and anecdotes in prose and free verse, at once touching and chilling. With pieces about David Ignatow, Allen Ginsberg, and H. R. Hays the book leaves a haunting lasting impression, like the poet's mother in "The

Hospital Chair"—"She touches you and tells you you are healed/ and may go home," but also warns "No one knows what will happen/ when I leave my tomb in the night/ to touch you". —**BRIAN CLEMENTS**, *Boog City*

Ernesta In the Style of the Flamenco

"*Ernesta, in the Style of the Flamenco,* Sandy McIntosh's latest volume, bursts with brilliance and sizzles with sass. McIntosh's new poems are audacious, ravishing, syntactic marvels, clowning-around oddballs. The energy and wit in this book will make you want to whip out your fan, put on your non-skid sole shoes, and dance".—**DENISE DUHAMEL**

"In *Ernesta,* when McIntosh's title character declares: 'Music has pictures,' it instantly brings to mind this poet's astounding use of language that creates visual landscapes of great clarity. I've been an enthusiastic fan of previous books and recommend you get your hands on as many as you can. This may be the biased sentiment of a devoted fan, but Sandy: You rock!" —**PHOEBE SNOW**